HEY BABY!

HEY BABY!

HEY BABY!

Sarah Bullen

For my mother and my daughter Ruby

CONTENTS

Acknowledgements

Dr Andrea Taub for the wonderful work she does with post-natal depression. Rachael Goldman and Freidy Yanover, Nicole Sacks on body matters and Boris Jivkov.

The sassy and very brilliant Sharon Marsay for changing the way so many women think about childbirth and for really doing incredible life-changing work with families.

The TM Centre in Houghton for hours of research time.

Tamsen, Beathur, Sharon, Carin, Beryl, the three Kims, Justine, Ilze-Marie, Nomsah and all the incredible women who shared their stories with such honesty.

Michelle Matthews for her support, creativity and her talent in writing and editing.

Anne Taylor, my editor, for keeping me on track.

The searingly brilliant Naomi Wolf for starting all my questions. When I read her first chapter of *Misconceptions* I cried for hours, and it was a book that started my journey of inquiry.

Beauty Moyo for loving my daughter so much and giving me the space to be out there in the world.

My parents Janeen and Eric, for their incredible love, support and friendship. I couldn't have chosen two more perfect parents for me.

Amanda Patterson at The Write Co for showing me that writers write.

Liz and Jayne for friendship, love and support I could only recreate in my dreams.

And finally, to my indescribably delicious husband Llewelyn, who is everything to me and more.

Experts

This book is the outcome of two years of information undertaken for the purpose of making a documentary and then writing a book. The information was collected through interviews and from medical journals, workshops, antenatal and post-natal classes, Internet websites, pamphlets, booklets, books, textbooks and magazines. While all effort has been made to credit information sources, omissions are made in error and are unintentional.

The following experts were consulted in writing this book:
Bev Voigt and Dr Vicky Broom on Vedic medicine and Maharishi Ayarveda.
Dr Kgalushi Koka on African rituals and rites.
Dr Vicky Broom on psychological issues around motherhood.
Keren Machanik for legal advice and contract law.
Nicole Sacks on diet and body matters.
Dr Andrea Taub on post-natal depression.
Rachael Goldman and Freidy Yanover on Jewish rites of passage.
Sharon Marsay and Cheryl Nikodem for pregnancy and birthing matters.
Dr Boris Jivkov on medical matters.
Dr Ronald Klein on childbirth and pregnancy.
Dr Debbie Cohen for physiotherapy advice.

Internet sources

Go Ask Alice www.goaskalice.com
Baby Zone www.babyzone.com
University of Columbia www.columbia.edu

ECureme www.ecureme.com

Midwifery www.midwifery.com

Explain Please www.explainplease.com

Plastic Surgery South Africa www.plasticsurgeons.co.za

The Association of Plastic and Reconstructive Surgeons of
Southern Africa www.plasticsurgery.co.za

Dr Patrick Hudson www.phudson.com

iVillage www.ivillage.co.uk

BabyCentre www.babycentre.co.uk

Mothers Who Think www.salon.com

Books and journals

Salt: A World History by Mark Kurlansky (Penguin)

Crying: The Natural and Cultural History of Tears by Tom Lutz
(WW Norton)

Candida Albicanus by Leon Chaitow (Thorsons)

New Atlas of Human Anatomy (Constable Publishers)

The Optimum Nutrition Bible by Patrick Holford (Platkus)

The Ultimate Weight Loss Solution by Dr Phil McGraw
(Free Press)

The Complete Guide to Post-Natal Fitness by Judy DiFiore
(A&C Black)

I Want Cosmetic Surgery, Now What? by Jodie Green
(Silver Lining Books)

The Complete Guide to Health and Well-being
(Greenwich Editions)

'Can Mothers Think?' by Jane Smiley (Greywolf Press)

Expectant Mothers Guide 2003 (Pampers booklet)

Recommended reading

Three in a Bed by Deborah Jackson (Bloomsbury)

Baby Bliss by Dr Harvey Karp (Penguin)

Parenting isn't for Cowards by Dr James Dobson
   (Multnomah Publishers)

What to Expect – The 1st Year by Dr Murkoff, (Eisenberg &
   Hathawne, Simon & Schuster)

Baby Sense by Anne Richardson and Megan Faure (Metz Press)

FabDad2 by Paul Kerton (Spearhead)

Misconceptions by Naomi Wolf (Chatto and Windus)

Homeopathy for the Home by Dr Ruth Block and
   Dr Barbara Lewis (Struik)

Homeopathy Encyclopaedia by Dr Gerard Pacaud
   (Hachette Illustrated)

Disclaimer

*This book does not replace medical advice. The opinions
are the author's own. Some names have been changed
to protect privacy.*

Foreword

There are few irreversible decisions in life and becoming a mother has got to be the greatest. But how could anyone, even our elders, prepare us for the transition that becoming a mother brings to our lives? It is a journey nobody can describe to you or explain, and it is one you walk alone. You give your whole body to carrying your child, and then it arrives and you are committed to raising it. You give your freedom, your career and soul to being a "good enough" mother.

For some moms, having a tiny baby that is totally dependent on them is the essence of fulfilment. For others, this can be a terrifying, lonely and confusing experience.

This book will help you realise that you aren't the only one feeling out of her depth and that you most certainly do not have to be perfect. It is hip, fun, hilarious and a must-read for any smart and sassy mother who is struggling through the social and intellectual desert that is the first year of motherhood. It is searingly honest and manages to take the medical and magical and incorporate both in the new world of motherhood.

You may feel that there is so much that you don't know. What you do know is that your child has hand-picked you. The ultimate joy of motherhood occurs when you stop resisting the opportunity of evolving with your new role and seize the chance to take a fresh look at your life and find a new space for yourself. This book takes you on that journey. It will make you laugh at yourself and your battle to come to terms with the dramatic change your life has taken. It will make you realise you are not alone, you are not mad; you are simply a new mom.

DR ANDREA TAUB

Dr Taub has worked solely in the field of treating and studying post-natal depression (PND) for the past six years. She is a frequent radio and magazine commentator and lectures on the condition.

HIP
MOM'S
swan
SONG

This is all very strange, but somehow it seems the most natural thing in the world to be lying stark naked in a strange bed with my nipple being gently rubbed between the fingers of another woman.

Okay, she is my midwife, but still, it would have been a bit odd just ten hours ago. Now I am neither excited nor embarrassed – I am pathetically grateful. Ten hours ago I was pregnant. Now I am a mother to a small and wet little brunette called Ruby. Eleven hours ago, I was snapping orders to my office over my cellphone while firing off an email. Now, I am a scared, humble woman. Nurses are gods; in fact, I am prepared to kneel before anybody who can cast some light on how to get my nipple to stay in this small otter's mouth. Who would have guessed the bad luck; that they are born not knowing how to suck?

Even my husband seems to know more than I do about it. He is certainly making enough suggestions and has attempted a new sophisticated one-handed technique of squeezing my breast between his index and third finger.

CHAPTER 1

WE ALL HAVE SOME SORT OF PICTURE OF LIFE WITH A BABY. I pictured a gorgeous little bundle whose eyes lit up when she saw me. I saw blonde curls and pink stockings and family holidays where we all baked and swam. I imagined her first birthday party with pale pink dry martinis for the guests and snow-white cupcakes for the kids. In short, I imagined a damned glamorous accessory.

My first inkling that I might have been a bit deluded came when a small brunette suddenly emerged from the water, like a mewling cat. Surely there is some mistake; my daughter is blonde. "That first cry," a fellow mom had said, emotionally, only days before, "is just about the best sound you will ever hear." She was then in the realm of 'experienced mom', having had her birth some two weeks before. I realised she could also have been hearing-impaired.

My husband was swishing her around in the birthing pool in the middle of our lounge cooing, "Ooooh, she is perfect."

I was staring at him in fascination thinking: "Someone has made a mistake. This is not what my child looks like." I was looking at a miniature version of my husband; I had expected a little me.

"Take her," ordered the midwife after some time. Somehow I knew "I'll pass," was not the response everyone was looking for.

This must be a bad movie. Somebody, please, press stop.

There are shelves of books about your baby. How to swaddle it into your own personal straightjacket, wipe its bum and extract boogers from its nose. How to breastfeed, massage its pressure points, how to burp it and what to give it for colic. But there is little advice on how to look after yourself, save a brief six-week visit with the obstetrician. There are tomes and libraries on what your baby should eat and weigh, but nothing on how slowly you

> *" I would never have got through the first three months without Eglanol, Bertha the night nurse and Infants Inc. "*

HIP MOM'S *swan* SONG

16

> *"With my first child, I had drug-free, natural birth and checked myself out the next day. My second was also totally natural, but I decided to stay the full three days permitted by the medical aid at the time. By my third, I had got the hang of things. I checked in for five days and got a full epidural. With two toddlers at home and fully aware of what the first few weeks are like with a newborn, I was going to take every second I could to relax in the hospital."*

will shrink or how many hours you will lie whimpering in shock over the downward spiral your life has taken. It is only in a candid moment, months later, that you will slip your Preparation H cream quietly into the outdoor bin and say goodbye to some of the horrific indignities you have glossed over during the last few months. Well, we quite like those horrific and hilarious moments here.

We are not interested in how you arrived home with a little tot. Sorry, but that's ancient history in this new life where every day turns you into a new African pioneer. (This time, you've got a Peg-a-Prego instead of an ox wagon.)

We are interested in how you are going to cope for the next twelve months. We are not yet even ready to talk about the rest of your life. In fact, we are not quite sure yet that this is any life.

Hot shot, now what?

One minute you are poring over Prada pumps, PDA in one hand and a vodka martini in the other, the next minute you are freezing your breast milk in a Jiffy bag and bulk-buying maxi-pads. It happens so fast and with such velocity that you are left open-mouthed and reeling. My fanny feels like I have been on a fourteen-day bareback Lesotho pony trail, my boobs have expanded from

> *"Over the last two days, my boobs and guava have seen more action than over the last six years of my marriage."*

A cup to EE in three days and it's not as much fun as I thought it would be. In fact, it's so not-fun it's scary. I have a pile of magazines beside my bed that make the assumption that I might be interested in making a decoupage changing table with an illustration of an Egyptian goose. Worst of all, everyone is talking to me in the third person and calling me 'mom'. As in: "Okay Mom, let's whip off our knickers, I am just going to take a quick look at Mom's labia."

All those nights of antenatal classes, the hours with magazines and books, the endless talk about being pregnant. Well, that's all over in a few hours, and then you are left with a dearth of information, bruised pudenda and a seriously outsized frame.

There is nothing that can prepare you for the initial shock of arriving home with a newborn baby, nor for the twelve months that follow that arrival – not the horror stories from vindictive friends who have been there and survived, not the glowing but misty memories of your mom, and most certainly, not the pregnancy magazines with tastefully soft-focus fanny shots and tubby moms with grimaces.

"Oh, I am already saying, it's not that bad. But then all new moms look at each other and smile – because we know it is that bad – but it does get better, slowly. And life does go on, it seems, on the surface."

You cannot give it back; you can't even let it out of your sight. From an ass-kicking career girl, you become incapable of even remembering whether you sleep during the day or at night. The answer is neither.

Everyone trots out the old saying that it takes a village to raise a child. Well, the only villages we have left in our walled suburban world are prefixed by the word 'retirement'. We have glossy bookstores with endless shelves on raising a baby. We have Google and chat rooms. We can pick up the phone and call a friend without getting up from the bed. We have our own tribes created around shopping malls and Sunday braais, but where the hell are the real villages when you need them? If I had found one, I certainly would have moved in.

Bacardi breeder

When you bring your baby home, the outpouring of love and support from people is overwhelming. Endless visitors want to look and cuddle, your vases run out and your champagne consumption reaches a lifetime high. The stream of visitors is endless and random. Former colleagues from ten years ago, friends, relatives, neighbours and former lovers, they all come and visit for a while. But they all leave. The rest of the time you are left alone, twenty-four hours a day and seven days a week, with your baby. You alone are there through the screaming and the sleeping and the agonized, wind-tortured faces. It's *Groundhog Day* and you are Bill Murray. You are there for every bath, every feed and every sleep. It never ends. And yes, there are times when you want to go mad.

And most of us have moments when we ask ourselves: "If I knew what it was going to be like, would I ever have done this?"

"Emotionally, I was totally blown away after the birth. Most of all, I felt somehow betrayed by my mother for not preparing me for the massive lifestyle change I was in for. I took it all out on her and one day just lay on the kitchen floor having what could only be described as an incredible tantrum out of sheer frustration."

" I got by the first three weeks on champagne. No matter what time I got a visitor, I would insist on toasting with a glass of champagne or two. I am by no means a drinker, but it was the only way I felt I could cope. In retrospect, I was probably trashed most of the time. Fortunately our bottle store delivers, but the bill was staggering."

In fact that question never left my mind for a full three months.

You are going to forget this time. It is going to disappear in a haze of romantic memories. It will only be after many tequilas and a candid conversation that your husband will dare to mention the snivelling misery you were after the birth.

Good looking mamma

Let's get one thing straight upfront. There is simply no way you can look good after childbirth. I would like to believe this is a truism for all moms. Anyone who tells you that you are looking your best is a lily-livered liar, so out them now.

"You look gooooood," one nurse crooned as I walked into the paediatrician's waiting room, six weeks postpartum. "No one would believe you had a baby just weeks ago." Now this is not the sort of thing I needed to hear. I need little encouragement to resort to taking my clothes off. Off came the kaftan and out of the closet came the string vests. A few days later, I was waiting at another reception when an anaesthetist I knew walked past. "Oooh," he enthused, "and when are you due?"

It's particularly difficult to look glowing and glamorous on your hands and knees in a steaming-hot bath, ass in the air, as you manhandle a lump out of your milk duct. And that's once you realise it is milk, not a terminal breast tumour that will leave your three-week-old motherless.

It's equally tough to look fine in a pair of drawstring pants and an outsize prairie girl top. Sarah Jessica Parker did it in three months, but she is superwoman and has two personal trainers and a chef shacked up in her Manhattan brownstone. I could not have lost the weight in twelve weeks even if I had had my jaws wired and a stomach bypass operation.

Welcome to the club. Now, first up, there are a few things you need to know. It's a club that is not exclusive. There are no heated towels or cocktails at the juice bar. This club is a club that is marked by soft bellies, bloodshot eyes and stretched perineums. But feel reassured that it's a club most women join at some point in their lives. And, fortunately, it's a club from which we all graduate.

Touched

I remember after Ruby's birth suddenly having incredible respect for any woman who had birthed a child. Gone were my judgements about the best way to give birth – which for me had entailed a large blue pool in the centre of our lounge. The sheer fact that it had been done was enough to earn massive respect. And that's what you get for the first few weeks after the birth. Respect. It's as if all practitioners, from midwives and nurses to cleaning staff, have lessons in authenticity. The routine is the

" When I first saw the photos of me and Lillian after the birth, I cried for hours with shock. I was blotchy and swollen with a burst blood vessel in my eye from the pushing. I insisted my husband reprint them in sepia, which was far more forgiving. "

" I was totally naïve. I lived out on a farm and had absolutely no clue what to do. When Keith was eight months he had had nothing but breast milk. Then my milk suddenly just dried up. I walked down to the shops, bought a litre of cow's milk and that's what he drank, diluted in a bit of water. We had no books in those days, and I had no mother. "

same with each. A long and meaningful look in the eye, a long squeeze of the arm and an affirmation: "Well done!"

Your arm is not the only place they squeeze repeatedly.

Get ready for a body blast that can blow you away. You are going to be prodded, poked, measured and squeezed by every passing nurse, doctor and a fair share of casual visitors.

"Oooh, please," a friend asked staring at my flaccid and floppy post-birth belly. "Can I just feel it?" Now I was the type of pregnant person who still sucked her stomach in when a hand shot towards it. Had he got it all wrong or was this some repressed childhood fetish? My wide-eyed look was taken as a go-ahead. I still wake sweating thinking of that moment.

Your breasts are going to be on public display with a pair of rosebud lips attached to them. Don't think the fact that your child is taking her tea will stop perfect strangers asking for a gander. "Just a sec, she's feeding," is no alibi. What's left to hide after you've had a baby?

" One of the most amazing things about motherhood is the support from other women who have children. It happens all the time and everywhere. I love how crossing this unseen bridge has allowed me in to the secrets I was never aware of. Or maybe, I just never saw all that support there before. "

Mommy myths

Only the first six weeks are tough: Motherhood is rougher than a cowboy's hand, but it can be as much fun. Having kids is hard going. You just get better at handling it.

Instinct will get you through: Not a chance. Sure you have an innate knowledge that you shouldn't offer it a sip of your G 'n T, or swing it around your head, but the rest does not come all that naturally. This is one time you are going to have to start reading the 'how to' books you thought were for dummies.

All women want to stay at home and look after their babies: Some people really do think this. Being a full-time mom has got to be the toughest job on the block. You will never work as hard as this. Going back to work is like taking a holiday compared to seven days a week of smiling and cooing.

Good mothers always put their babies first: This only happens for the first few months. Then you realise that your relationship comes first and you come somewhere too.

Having a baby will bring your relationship closer: Life will quickly prove you wrong. In fact, children are guaranteed to put your marriage under serious strain. What with fatigue, stress,

"I have accepted that life is now different, that my time is not my own. But today, there is no handbrake to the slide. It is rage and anger and frustration at this little thing. Not her, but the change she has forced on my life. I would not trade it for all the world, but it is impossibly huge at times."

low libido and resentment you are never going to have to work harder on your relationship than when you have kids.

I can do it differently: Well you do try, but sooner or later you will drop the desire to breastfeed until they are four, give them a daily massage with sesame oil and stimulate their brains into being the next Mark Shuttleworth. Then it's toast and jam like the rest of the mothers you thought were lazy slackers.

The first five days

These are the most glorious and the toughest. You and your body go though huge changes as your hormones rebalance and your milk comes in.

Day one: You are on cloud nine. Your baby is ten hours old and you have not slept a wink in over twenty-four hours. You cannot stop staring at this incredible bundle of creation. It is so beautiful it's breathtaking. You are working hard at getting it to latch on to your nipple.

Day two: You are in a love cocoon with the new family. All three of you have spent the last forty-eight hours in bed, just loving each other. You have had forty-five minutes' sleep but feel like you don't need any sleep at all.

" *I think we let people through the door one weekend, about ten days after my son arrived and I remember looking at this scene of normality with people chatting and laughing and drinking tea in my house like I had landed on an alien planet. The whole world was a new place to me.* "

Day three: Still no sleep. Your milk is coming in and the skin of your breasts is stretched so taut you think it may split. The nurses say it won't. Baby is latching, but it's no relief. You have been crying for three hours now and your partner said he was going for a short walk an hour ago. You have left seventeen messages on his cellphone.

Day four: You are back at home so maybe you will get some sleep. Surely the human body cannot go indefinitely without sleep. Can it? You count each hour to the midwife's next visit. Baby must have colic. It just won't stop crying.

Day five: Three hours sleep. Oh bliss! But now you've tasted release, you want more. Baby is feeding every hour so that's not possible. There's a flashing dot on your bedside clock and you've been counting the ticks for the last hour. Each feed takes 800 ticks.

TYPES OF MOM:
IDENTIFY YOURSELF

THE CLINGY MOM

It's been eight months and baby has only left your sight for a few hours at a stretch. You have given up work; you have given up all interests. All you can talk about is your child. You wonder why friends are avoiding your calls.

THE OVERPROTECTOR

You do the Heimlich every time your darling gags and have heard of three babies that have been snatched from Hyde Park Exclusive Books. You wonder why other babies are crawling around like beetles on Red Bull. Your baby prefers to be held close to you all day.

THE SUPER-ORGANISER

Colour-coded Tupperware, dummy clips, travel packs of baby wipes and spare food jars are your focus. You have everything on hand. You spend your weekend pre-cooking and packaging batches of food for each weekday. You have forgotten what used to consume your time before you had a baby.

THE NEW AGE FAIRY

Your baby is still sleeping in your bed at eleven months and waking most of the night. You don't believe in routine and want the baby to develop its own rhythm with life. You know she is a crystal soul. You are very tired.

THE CAREER GAL

Back at work on week six. Your life cannot stop despite your husband's grumblings. Your mom knows better than to say a word. It's tough, but you need to do this for your sanity. You wonder why your child is so needy during your precious weekend time with him.

THE HIP MOM

Baby is on a strict routine sleeping through the night and you are back in your size tens within three months. Everyone tells you how calm and serene you are. You are running your business from home. You are in tears by five every evening and think you may not make the year.

THE PROFESSIONAL

Babies and birthing are the focus of your world. You know it's boring, but you just can't help yourself. You dispense advice on everything from weight to teething ratios. You smile knowingly when friends talk about their lives and say: "Just you wait until you have a baby." Dinner invitations are dwindling.

my story: Carin

There I was, a respectable thirty-something woman seen between various social functions driving my red convertible Mercedes, clad in micro-minis and high-heeled shoes, groomed, sussed, savvy and thinking of myself as, well, glamorous. And then I fell pregnant. My glad-rags were replaced by drawstrings and elasticised waists. Everything was big, including me. My glamour was reduced to pumps and a handbag.

But it was the day that I packed a hospital bag that I finally bade farewell to my glamour. My passport to my new life was in the form of a maternity pad. I had never seen something so large. Was it my newborn or me who would be donning a nappy? And how was this supersized panty-liner ever going to fit into my lacy G-string?

The actual birth was a series of acupuncture needles and internal examinations by my midwife until I eventually ended up on the slab. There I lay, with my gown around my neck, my legs splayed while my audience of fifteen pondered over my barely intact dignity. Fortunately, the anaesthetic numbed more than just my nerves, and I received my newborn with maternal delight.

When my vagina was through with all the action, we moved on to my breasts (more like the pendulous bosom of a porn star now). Day three saw more than the arrival of my milk supply – it saw my breasts getting more action than they had seen in the last thirty years. The midwives milked me like a bovine, kneading, squeezing, stroking and poking to get the milk supply flowing. But my breasts' appearances did not end there. They were still to go public. It was a clumsy relationship between nipple and lips – neither fully in control of the moment. Nevertheless, several months down the line, I have joined the ranks of the veterans and watch the new girls on the block fumbling with the act. Now, with my weight doing the slowest possible disappearing act, I have re-engaged an element of glamour – just as long as you overlook the Preparation H suppositories in my clutch bag and the milky deposit on my shoulder.

my story: Mandy

I felt no incredible bond with my baby. I glared at him without any emotion. This was the creature who caused me so much discomfort. I never bothered to think about my struggle to conceive or the fact that I was so overjoyed when I was told the 'good news' of my pregnancy. It was as though I was a different woman. There was no resemblance to the woman who faithfully attended all her prenatal appointments, who watched with fascination as her tummy enlarged month by month. In her place was a cold-hearted monster who regarded the poor defenseless soul as the reason for her painful and animal-like experience.

My husband got what he wanted: a son. I, on the other hand, felt so empty. I had never anticipated that the final moment of my pregnancy would end in such a negative way. I suppose I was not emotionally prepared for the severing of the umbilical cord. When he was safely inside my womb, he was mine alone. I felt his movements and I communicated with him. In a sick way, I blamed the baby for making his appearance at a time when I did not want him to. I wanted the link to last a little bit longer.

I suppose I became so obsessed with the living being inside of me, that I never thought a time would come when I had to say goodbye and allow him to live without my assistance.

I felt betrayed by this life. I was his incubator, his reason for surviving for nine months, and now he no longer needed me. He could breathe on his own, he could cry and others could hear, touch, stroke and comfort him. In essence, my own selfishness made me blind to the fact that he still needed me.

my story: Fatima

During the first few months, all I wanted was for time to move on. I didn't feel at all like a mother; I felt like a caretaker. There was no bond. There was just the endless drudge of keeping a little person alive. That's really all it is in the early days. What we forget is that the business of keeping another person alive is no mean feat. I didn't hate or resent Seth at all. I adored the idea of him. I loved the feel of him. I simply forgot to stay in those adoring, loving moments and spent far too much time guessing fluid quantities and assessing dirty nappies.

I think the worst part for me was the loneliness I felt. None of my friends had babies. I felt so out of touch with the world. I would emerge from the house and feel desperate to escape my little boy for a couple of hours, just to recapture that feeling of not having a baby to worry about. I couldn't bring myself to leave him, yet I was dying to get the hell away from him. I couldn't imagine things ever improving; I just imagined this black hole of motherhood that would chase me around for the rest of my life.

Of course, that is exactly what it does. I still struggle to see myself as a mother. I just want to be Fatima. Not Mom, Ma, Mama or anything else that sounds old and frumpy. I take Seth for walks in his pram and I can imagine people looking through me. They see this package – a mother and her son. My vanity misses being seen as a woman. Perhaps one day I'll start realising that I am now a mother and that this is an addition to the CV, not an eraser that obliterates all previous achievements. It's a helluva thing, motherhood, and it gets a lousy rap for all the right reasons.

WOMBS, BOOBS

and

OTHER THINGS THAT MOVE

I must have missed the class on the endless indignities visited upon a mother in the first few weeks after she gives birth. I can only think I must have nipped out to the loo during the session on losing all human pride. I certainly missed the bit about losing most of my friends and crying so long and so hard that even I got bored with myself.

I remember taking copious notes on every stage of labour ("I am moving into transition, this is the toughest part", I clearly hear myself saying on my birth video). I knew how to rock and moan, how to care for the cord (dust with homeopathic Wicusun powder). I had a freezer-full of homemade organic barley juice for stamina and had drawn up a room map of where every calming lavender candle would be placed.

I had followed, to the letter, those handy lists of what to have for baby. There, hand-washed, folded and ironed were the hooded towels, the Babygro's, beanies and blankets. But nothing for me, save six pairs of granny knickers. I had assumed that I would be looking after my new baby not that I might need to look after myself.

CHAPTER 2

I REALISED, ABOUT TEN MINUTES AFTER THE BIRTH, that things might not be going to plan as I lay on my lounge floor watching my midwife's busy hands. A pool of blood spread around me. I had never seen so much blood, certainly not in my house. "Thank heavens we decided not to carpet the lounge," I thought dreamily. A fleeting thought passed through my mind that I might be dying.

The barley juice was turfed out weeks later, untouched. I didn't notice the lavender candles – I doubt that even a horse dart would have been effective in calming me. In fact, a full CNN news crew could have been in the room, and I would have been none the wiser. Months later, my husband turned to me with misty eyes as he hummed along to *Vira: Melodic Panflute Vol II.* "This is Ruby's song," he said.

I looked at him blankly.

"It was playing when she was born..." he prompted.

"There was music?" I asked.

I had no notes on needing to pee every time I laughed, on bursting a vein in my eye, or on the feeling of having a fanny more bruised than the day I lost my grip on the jungle gym and landed on the crossbar. I'd had a dim vision during my daydreams months before of looking glamorous, champagne in hand, perhaps in a stylish pink organza kimono, as my house filled with friends and flowers. Crawling on all fours for three days and hiding from relatives for fifteen minutes in the downstairs guest loo was not in my picture.

" *I had not got out of bed for three days after my C-section when my friend Cat marched into the room. She dragged me out of bed and slapped a Voltaren suppository in my hand. 'Either you do it or I do,' she ordered. Ten minutes later, I was charging around. It gave me a kickstart.* "

" I got so constipated I had to have a colonic three times a day, crouching in the hospital bath to try and flush the massive blockage out of my intestines and bowel. It was ten days before I finally got it out and my body was in contractions like labour, to expel the massive foreign object. "

This is the part of childbirth that obstetricians gloss over with a wink during those exciting monthly visits, that midwives warmly tell you they will discuss with you"... when you are there".

Is this a secret society or the rest of my life you forgot to mention?

Your entire life has changed in a few short hours and your body has just gone through nine months of pregnancy and a birth. Not only is your body fighting to recover, your physical state is, strangely, not the focus of your attention. You are in pain, bruised, swollen and maybe stitched. You may have had major surgery. You have lost a lot of blood. Your hormones are raging and your body is in shock. But you don't have time to think of that as you are getting to grips with a suckling leach.

It's a confusing time. So many things are going on that it's difficult to tell what is normal and what is not. We are going to clear that up right away so you know what is happening to your body over the first six weeks after you give birth.

" I woke up after only an hour's nap to find totally different breasts. My size A's had become EE cups and were growing by the minute. They were alabaster white with blue veins streaking across them, like a scene from Interview With a Vampire. They were magnificent but aching like hell. "

THE FOURTH TRIMESTER

The critical period of recovery and the processes your body will go though in the six weeks after the birth is medically described as puerperium. It is actually the fourth trimester of pregnancy. If you think you are back to normal, think again girlfriend.

Technically, this period of physical recovery starts with the delivery of the placenta and ends when your uterus returns to its non-pregnant state, usually around six weeks.

This six-week period is tumultuous, profound and terrifying for many women. You are battling raging hormones, chronic sleep deprivation, extreme mood swings, helplessness, tears, bruising, pain and often stitches and surgical wounds. It is a time of self-doubt, extreme anxiety, nightmares and fear. Or it's a time of a blissful haze as you cuddle with your baby. Every mother must travel this journey in her own way.

Bear in mind that this will come to an end in time. You will look back with amazement at the journey you have been through. For many women, the first few weeks are a baptism of fire into a new life, a rebirth of self. It is a fight for the old life and the eventual acceptance of a new life.

The six-week or 42-day period is honoured in many cultures as a time when the baby and mother are secluded and given a chance to recover. You are more fragile than you think. Your heart is wide open and your life has changed irrevocably. Friends can wait. In-laws will not take offence. Your baby is going to be around for a long time for everyone to visit. Take all the time you need to honour yourself for the bravery of the tremendous journey you have taken. Honour your body for its courage and strength. Honour it with time, rest and tenderness. Honour your heart for its huge capacity for love that you are just starting to glimpse.

The involution starts here

The second your baby and placenta are delivered a remarkable chain of events is set in motion that will result in your uterus shrinking by a thousand per cent in six weeks. The process is called involution.

The uterus, or womb, is considered the strongest muscle in the human body. It is ingeniously designed to accept a baby, then carry it to term and deliver it. What's more, it's designed to do it over and over again.

When it starts the push to get your baby out it also launches its return to pre-pregnancy size. Muscular contractions are triggered by the hormone oxytocin that floods your body during labour. Once your baby and placenta are delivered, the thick muscular wall of the uterus still has some serious work to do. It will continue to contract, relax, contract and relax until it has reduced.

The interior wall of the uterus is the site of a large blood clot where the placenta was attached to the muscle. This area is rich in blood vessels so the organ needs to shrink fast, to reduce the amount of surface area that can bleed.

- By week forty, the top of the uterus (fundus) is sitting somewhere near your diaphragm. It's taken nine months to get to that size.
- Your uterus starts to contract during labour.
- Immediately after delivery, it is the size of a large mango and weighs around 1 000 grams.
- By week two, the top of the fundus should be back down in your pelvic cavity, and the uterus will weigh around 300 grams.
- By week six, the uterus should have returned to its non-pregnant state, with a weight of around fifty to seventy grams, around the size of a large lime.

" I was fine for the first week and then the shock hit. By 4pm every day I had reached the end of the road. As my husband came through the door, the tears and hysteria started. I just couldn't hold it in. "

> *"Far more than the birth, the ongoing and heavy bleeding distressed me. I just wanted it all over and here I was, contending with what felt like litres of blood draining out of me. I have never been squeamish, but I lost three litres of blood at the birth and the psychological effect of the heavy bleeding made me feel like I was somehow, slowly, dying even though I knew it was really okay."*

- Your uterus is a muscle and will never quite regain its pre-pregnancy tone.
- Involution is most efficient with your first baby. With subsequent babies, your uterus will have lost muscle tone.
- If you are not breastfeeding, your periods will resume six to eight weeks after delivery.

What kinda sore are we talking?

> *"I was standing one morning with my midwife in my kitchen. As I made her a cup of tea, she was mashing a blood clot the size of a grapefruit with my kitchen fork. It felt fairly normal."*

- The cramping will be most intense during the first 24 to 48 hours after giving birth and can resemble mild to moderate labour or a menstrual cramp.
- The discomfort should taper off within two to three days and come to an end by six weeks.
- Don't be alarmed if you don't feel it particularly with your first baby. It is happening.
- The contraction starts most powerfully as your baby first latches and starts to feed.
- Breastfeeding stimulates the process and cramping can become significant while you nurse.
- Cramping will be more severe with subsequent babies as your muscle has lost tone and will have to work harder to get back into shape.

Can I help my uterus, ahem, involute?

Breastfeed: The suckling process stimulates oxytocin (see Know Your Hormones, pg 40). The downsizing of your uterus will start immediately whether you breastfeed or not, but breastfeeding will help your body kick it into a higher gear.

Massage your uterus: See box, pg 39.

Don't hold it in: A full bladder will work against the contracting mechanisms.

Relax: Your body is on autopilot, and this process will happen naturally.

So, what's all this blood about?

Postpartum bleeding is called lochia. If you think this sounds like a small Scottish lake, you are not too far off track. It refers to the alarmingly heavy vaginal bleeding that will occupy your waking hours in between breastfeeds and burping. If you are at all tempted to leave the house, the crackling noise as the voluminous maxipads rub between your thighs will put you off public appearances.

"I passed a clot the size of a grapefruit ten days after the birth. I was so shocked when I put my hand down to feel what was in my pants that I went into a state of extreme trauma and uncontrollable shaking. Fortunately, my mom was with me and handled it all like a pro. We called my obstetrician and he said that it was totally okay, but I need to show him. We kept it in the fridge in some plastic wrap until our visit the next day."

WOMBS, BOOBS *and* OTHER THINGS THAT MOVE

WHAT IS IT?

Residual bleeding from the placental scar site. The fluid is made up of mucus, blood and tissue. As the bleeding tails off, the discharge will be made up of the inner lining of the uterus as it sheds.

Days one to five: Expect fresh, heavy blood *(lochia rubra)*. Expect to use up to two maternity pads at a time, changing them every two to three hours.

Days five to thirty: The bleeding should start to tail off. The blood content will diminish, and the discharge will become pinker.

Day thirty onwards: The discharge will move to an opaque white colour.

WHAT ABOUT CLOTS?

Clots are a normal part of healing and you will pass clots that vary in size from a grape to an egg. The site of the placenta doesn't just scar over and be done during involution, otherwise its surface area would be a thick scab and would not allow future eggs to attach. The tissue underneath actually heals, pushing the scab away and it forms part of your vaginal bleeding (lovely lochia).

These can often gather overnight and all appear at one time as you get up and gravity works its wonders. Any clot larger than an egg you need to keep. Your caregiver needs to check that there are not pieces of the placenta still left in your uterus. These can cause infection and hold back involution.

TIP

Don't even think about using a tampon.

Call your doc for:

- **Intense pain:** You should feel a cramp, not a sharp pain.
- **Heavy bleeding:** If you are using more than a pad an hour. The quantity of blood should not be more than a very heavy period.
- **A smell:** Any smelly discharge can indicate infection. You will be put on antibiotics, fast, by your doctor.

MASSAGE YOUR UTERUS:

- Lie down and relax your abdominal muscles.
- Feel below your navel for the top of the uterus (fundus).
- It will be sensitive to the touch, bordering on painful.
- Massage downwards, using medium to heavy pressure.
- Use breathing techniques to relax and flow with the pain.
- Do not tense your abdominal muscles.
- Even if you can't find your uterus, it's there – so just massage downwards from your navel to your pubic bone.

It also helps to put gentle pressure on the area. Try lying on your stomach with a pillow under the lower stomach.

KNOW YOUR HORMONES

OXYTOCIN

This steroid hormone is nothing short of magical. Released in the brain, oxytocin moves down to your pituitary gland and then enters your bloodstream where it travels to tissues as distant as the uterus. Oxytocin works on several tissues but most specifically on genital, uterine and vaginal tissues. It is the catalyst that stimulates the muscles in the walls of your womb to contract during childbirth. It will continue to stimulate your uterus to contract for the next six weeks. It is also known as the "cuddle hormone". It's the hormone that is triggered when your genitals are stimulated and its levels increase five-fold before orgasm when it stimulates mild contractions (like a small pumping action) of your uterus and fallopian tubes. These little flutters actually promote conception.

The hormone also triggers lactation and prompts the 'let down' reflex. It is responsible for helping individuals forge strong emotional bonds. Mothers often have an overwhelming feeling of love with this hormone coursing through their veins. It can be directed at your partner, not necessarily your child.

PROGESTERONE

This is a steroid hormone and its levels vary over your reproductive cycle. As its name suggests (pro-gestation) it's critical to pregnancy and nursing. Its volumes are highest during pregnancy as it works to relax the muscle tissue in your body. It causes your ligaments to stretch and every fibre to become more pliable. It works to normalise or restore changes to the body caused by oestrogen. These effects include normalising blood clotting and vascular tone, zinc and copper levels, cell oxygen levels and use of fat stores for energy.

Hurricane hormone

The placenta is both the seat of your baby's life and the most powerful hormone delivery system to your body. After you deliver this, the change in your hormones is nothing short of spectacular.

- Within three hours of delivery, the level of oestrogen in your body will have dropped by a staggering ninety per cent. This is the hormone that encourages your cells to retain water, to stretch and to relax. Its quick decline will start a process of water elimination from your body that is discussed later in the chapter.
- Within three days, oestrogen will have reached pre-pregnancy levels, a tenfold reduction over three days.
- As your oestrogen drops, you will get a surge of oxytocin. This hormone starts flooding into your body in buckets during labour and birth.

The incredible change in your hormone levels will take an emotional toll as well. You will feel overwhelmed and weepy. Combine that with debilitating fatigue and physical exhaustion and the term "baby blues" makes it sound trite in the extreme. You may find yourself weeping buckets watching the Discovery Channel or slumped snivelling on the floor as a visitor arrives. A combination of sleep deprivation, hormones gone berserk and

" I had what seemed like hundreds of visitors. I would sit in what looked like my lounge with faces I knew were my friends, but I was in an alien world of endless sleepless nights and bottomless tears. "

the sudden overwhelming responsibility of this little baby, all crash down on you.

Added to that, you may be contending with pain, bruising, stitches, the remnants of heavy analgesic drugs knocking around in your liver and meddling in-laws who could rock the centered soul of the Dalai Llama.

Waterworks

From the moment of the birth, your body is trying to shed the excess water it accumulated during pregnancy. The fluid stored by your body is rapidly being eliminated through your blood stream and lymphatic system. Over the next few days, your body will eliminate two to four litres of water. There are only two channels it can use – sweat and urine. Sweating increases when you breastfeed.

Your body, particularly your kidneys, is working like a pressure cooker to get things back under control and your bladder is the rather small outlet valve.

It will take two to eight weeks for your bladder to recover completely, and about seven per cent of women develop stress incontinence after delivery. If you act quickly and give it the best chance of recovery, your likelihood of getting off scot-free increases.

" I find myself getting teary just hearing others' birth stories or reading testimonies online. "

Let's be frank. Your bladder may never be quite the same again. (Another secret your antenatal lecturer forgot to mention?) Its supporting muscles may have taken a serious knock with the pressure of a long pregnancy. All your pelvic organs were under huge and sustained pressure from the pregnancy and then additional pressure from the actual birth.

BLADDER DO'S AND DON'TS

- **Don't hold it in:** This is not the time to test your control. A full bladder is going to add additional strain to a stretched muscle and can impair the contractions of your uterus. Bedpan, catheter or the good old john, just get it out.
- **Do empty your bladder completely.**
- **Don't stop drinking water:** Ironically, drinking water helps reduce water retention, not increase it.
- **Do start Kegel exercises as soon as you can:** A few hours after birth is not too soon and forever is not long enough.

"Those first few weeks are a time apart from all reality. It is just you; a tiny, mewling little alien; and an endless box of tissues."

KIDNEYS: CLEAN BEAN

Your kidneys are the organs that cleanse your body's blood.

Only seven centimetres long, they hold twenty-five per cent of your blood at any given time.

Every minute over a litre of blood passes through them. They process 1 500 litres a day and clean all the blood in your entire body every fifty minutes.

The kidneys pass urine to your bladder. They can store two cups of liquid at a time and generally fill up and need to be emptied every three to four hours. During a 24-hour period, you will produce 1.5 litres of liquid.

Just a jump to the left

Most of your internal organs are moving back into place fast.

They've shifted upwards, sideways or to the back to make room for your growing uterus and your baby. Suddenly, that mass has gone and your organs can't wait to get back to where they belong. Acid reflux will stop immediately, but expect a lot of farts and rumblings as your intestines drop back down into your belly cavity and things start to shift back into place.

Your pulse rate returns to its pre-pregnancy rate in one or two days and the increased volume of blood returns to normal levels in approximately a week.

By week six, your cardiovascular system will be back to normal, which is when you will be given the go-ahead to exercise vigorously.

Bummer

Having just done the biggest push of their lives, most women are not keen to flex their sphincter muscle ever again. Some new mothers go the next morning like clockwork, but other women won't have a bowel movement for the first two to three days. A number of factors fuel a possible sphincter lock including inactivity or bed rest, drugs, dehydration, fear and hormones.

"After three days of no bowel action, I wanted a fast solution. A laxative suppository did the trick and then I moved on to longer-term remedies."

If you are prone to constipation keep a close eye on this. Don't wake up when ten days have passed and you are facing A Serious Situation.

Constipation must be avoided at all costs and you need to act quickly with a stool softener or laxative to get things moving.

See Chapter 3 for fast-acting and longer-term remedies.

TIP

Stay away from a dummy for the first two weeks. Your baby needs all the food he or she can get. It's exhausting business sucking that hard and you don't want to waste that energy, especially if you have engorged breasts that need relief through regular emptying.

Hello Dolly

Every part of your body, except your breasts, will start downsizing.

They will start by producing the first milk, colostrum, which will last for two to four days. This clear, almost salty liquid supplies your baby with antibodies and a bit of nosh to tide it over. But colostrum is not food and your baby will drop weight over the first forty-eight hours as it perfects its latching and lets your breasts know how much milk it needs. And then suddenly ... Wham. Some prankster attached a tank of helium to your boobs and hit full throttle. Your breasts realise what they were born to do: produce milk.

EXPECT:

- Engorgement. Phwoar! Yes.
- Totally lopsided breasts.
- Lumps the size of an apricot.

CALL THE DOC IF:

- A section of either breast feels hot, hard and tender to the touch.
- You have a fever.

TIP

Your husband is going to want to try a suckle at some time, poor boy. Be gentle.

Infections are common in the early days of breastfeeding as bacteria can enter the body through the milk ducts. These will be treated with antibiotics.

What if I'm not Mother Milk?

Choosing not to breastfeed or having to abandon breastfeeding is an emotional event and the first week will be a painful one as your oxytocin withdraws and, eventually, your milk dries up. You will not escape the first few days of engorgement before your lactation ends, but there is medication on the market to make your milk dry up faster.

There are two types of "anti-hormone" pills available. Both work to counteract the hormones in your body and are available on prescription.

Bromocriptine (trades as Parlodel) is an older, nevertheless effective, drug. It requires a course of a week to ten days of medication.

Cabergoline (trades as Dostinex) is a newer generation drug and a single tablet is effective in drying up your milk.

To decrease the chance of engorgement:

- Wear a tight-fitting bra or sports bra as soon after delivery as possible.
- Do not stimulate your breasts in any way, whether through massage, friction or hot showers.

" I was up and doing sit-ups on day three after my C-section. I felt great. "

Your milk should dry up within two weeks after giving birth. If you decide to reverse your decision, contact your caregiver as your breasts can be stimulated to produce milk again.

> " *I still feel that I missed out on something spectacular after both my boys (now ten and twelve) were delivered by C-section. Every time I hear new moms relate the stories of their deliveries, I get a feeling of disappointment that I never felt that primal, life-changing transition, even though there was no chance of a natural delivery.* "

Recovering from a C-section

Your experience of a C-section can be a blissful relief or a traumatic change of tack and chances are your recovery will reflect your degree of surprise at ending up on the metal slab.

Planned or not, if you are recovering from a C-section birth, doctors maintain that you are in for a significantly longer recovery time. Caesarean births are much safer now, but they still bear a higher risk than natural deliveries.

This is firstly due to risk of infection, and it is why the hospital stay after a Caesarean birth is usually twice as long as after a vaginal birth (usually three or four days). There are two types of incisions and scars – a "bikini" or a vertical midline incision. A vertical incision is a far safer operation carrying a lower risk of infection, but it is cosmetically less appealing, leaving you with a scar that runs from belly button to pelvis.

The second risk is from the anaesthesia. Although spinal anaesthetics have increased dramatically in safety over the last five years, a C-section has a fifteen times higher maternal death rate than natural delivery. Your body is under the influence of significant drugs that control your vital functions such as your blood pressure and heart function. Obstetricians agree that a planned C-section is safer than an emergency event. This is mainly due to the fact that obstetricians have their choice of anaesthetist and nurses if it is planned, whereas you may not be getting the

> " *I could not fathom the pain of my second C-section. I was on morphine but nothing could take away the intensity. It obscured all other emotions.* "

best possible staff at 3am on a Sunday.

- Post-operative infection will be swiftly treated with anti-biotics.
- You have had major surgery and now is a good time to respect your body and take as much time as you need to let it heal.
- You will be under medical care and closely monitored, but take responsibility for your own health and ask questions.
- Talk about how it all ended up. You may be contending with anger towards your doctor and feelings of inadequacy or disappointment. Or you may just feel relief that both you and your baby came through safely. It's important to discuss with your obstetrician why the decision for surgery was made and to realise that close to twenty per cent of births do not go according to plan.

From C to sexy

- **Get up and moving:** Get out of bed and start walking around the corridors as soon as you can. This will get the drugs moving out of your system and start your metabolism going. New mothers used to be under house arrest for six weeks, but increasing numbers of obstetricians say exercising will boost your healing capacity. We are not talking putting on your running shoes, more like taking a stroll to the shop.

"My midwife said I should just get into bed with Seth and let him feed almost constantly to keep the pressure down. It sounded good in theory but he was a lacklustre sucker and still battling to latch, so I ended up lying in a wet patch that covered the entire bed and boobs just spurting milk on their own."

- **Get adequate pain relief:** There are no prizes for martyrs. The most commonly prescribed drug for post-operative pain relief is Voltaren (Diclofanac). You have the choice of taking either a pure anti-inflammatory or a painkiller. A painkiller is a cocktail of drugs that will combine anti-inflammatory and pain-relief medications and is more effective in pain relief. Painkillers do, however, carry side-effects such as drowsiness or constipation. Your safest bet, as in pregnancy, is paracetemol (Panado). Avoid any drug with codeine – it's a morphine derivative and opiate and should not be taken while pregnant or nursing. Avoid aspirin as it has a powerful blood-thinning capacity and carries an increased risk of postpartum bleeding. Time your doses so they are not directly before you breastfeed.

- **Easy on the cookies:** More sophisticated analgesics mean you are no longer on a liquid diet for a week after a C-section. But still, the drugs used during surgery will temporarily paralyse your intestines so you are at even greater risk of constipation. Your primary concern is avoiding constipation. A few hours after surgery, attempt to swallow some sips of water. When you can tolerate liquids, without significant nausea or vomiting, move to a semi-solid, like soup. When all that stays down and you have passed a bowel movement easily, move on to soft, solid foods. Rumbling in the stomach and intestines is a good sign and means there is movement and your stomach function is starting up again.

" We had a waterproof sheet on our bed for the first six months. I produced so much milk that I would wake every night in a cold wet patch of milk from it just leaking out. "

WOMBS, BOOBS *and* OTHER THINGS THAT MOVE

TIP

Place one of your baby's waterproof sheets on your bed where you will sleep and breastfeed. It saves you having to replace the mattress later on.

Take a bow

No matter how your birth turned out, the most important thing is that you and your baby are safe and healthy. This is a triumph. We are so sanitised with modern medical management that it's easy to forget that you have just lived through a monumental physical achievement. Not only should the physical risk of the birth be honoured but also the fact that your body has grown, nurtured and held a baby for nine months and delivered it safely. Your heart has fed its heart and you have held it in a space of incredible love. It's nothing short of spectacular.

Motherhood is a massive, tough, exhilarating emotional vortex. It never ends, but you get better at handling it.

WARNING SIGNS

CALL YOUR OBSTETRICIAN IF YOU EXPERIENCE ANY OF THE FOLLOWING:

- Fever with a temperature of 38°C/100.4°F or above.
- Increased pain, swelling, redness or discharge from your episiotomy or Caesarean-section incision.
- Soaking through more than one sanitary pad an hour.
- Smelly discharge.
- Passing apricot-sized clots.
- Tender, warm, reddened breasts.
- A burning feeling when you pee.
- Increased swelling in legs or arms.
- Any unusual pain.

Trust yourself. If you think things are not okay, act fast.

BODY SHOTS:
DEALING WITH WHAT CAN GO WRONG

Berman & Berman sounds like a law firm based in downtown Chicago, but it's a thriving and very public centre, run by two meticulously groomed Los Angeles blondes. They specialise in sexual health for women. In fact, so popular are these two docs that they have a daily show.

"Hi," they start every show, "I'm Jennifer Berman and I'm Laura Berman. We are Berman and Berman."

Now, finding enough material to fill a weekly talk show is regarded as tough, but these girls talk about vaginas daily. Not just vaginas. Genitals. Dr Laura Berman saves you the embarrassment of asking by mentioning that this collective noun covers your labia, vagina, clitoris and vulva. And while men are intimate with every twist and turn of their packages, what's the bet that you are not quite sure where one of these ends and the other begins? We women have a strangely distant relationship with our genitals. Granted, they are not hanging around waiting for our constant scrutiny and loving touch, but even cursory fanny gazing is not an activity many of us rate highly. Which is strange, bearing in mind the massive emotional role they play in our lives. We know every bump and hair on our feet, but not a thing about our fannies.

CHAPTER 3

BERMAN AND BERMAN ARE OUT TO CHANGE THAT.
They want to talk about our genitals. They even want to talk about their genitals, which can be disturbing as they sit on their Martha Stewart set with power-suits and highlighted bobs. In fact Berman and Berman want to talk about anything to do with sex. Is it X-rated television? Is it even sexy? Definitely not. In fact, *Oprah* probably has more graphic content and – aside from the 'adults only' warnings – this show would not be amiss in an afternoon children's show line-up alongside *Learning Master Math*. Which goes to show that our vaginas are really two things at once: they are anatomical body parts and they are emotional, sensual and sexual triggers.

Being postpartum means you have to clearly separate these two functions, and this applies to all body parts, not just genitals. You need to put the emotional, spiritual and sexual to one side and you need to be clear that your body is also a functioning machine. It is a meticulously designed, intuitive and perfectly accurate machine. In other words, now is not the time to get precious about embarrassing bits. Just get them fixed. Sex and sexuality will return. But right now, you need to treat your body as a body, not as a metaphysical entity.

Be clear that your supporters will do just that. From nurses to obstetricians, they are interested in getting your body functioning properly no matter how embarrassing the part that is malfunctioning. It's not easy when your obstetrician is massaging your cervix or measuring the rate of your urine projectile, but think of yourself as a car in for a tune-up. Try to think sleek red Ferrari, not rusty Beetle.

Few women get away without complications after birth. Most just don't talk about them; they deal with them. You have a baby to look after so you'd better handle whatever is handed you without a grimace and get back to your baby.

SIX RULES FOR HEALTH

1. Trust your gut. If something does not feel right, don't ignore it.

2. Don't feel any guilt about calling a midwife or obstetrician at any time of day or night if you have any urgent concerns. They are not doing you a favour: this is their job.

3. Don't self-diagnose or suffer in silence. The chances are everything is normal, but a quick call to your doctor will put your mind at rest.

4. Choose how much you share with your partner. There are many other people you can talk to if you feel intimate discussions on incontinence may be too much. Try your mother, a friend or your family doctor.

5. Get a second opinion. The most important opinion is your own. There are as many solutions as there are problems. Go online and do some research. Talk to people who have done things differently then find your own way.

6. Act fast. Healthy or not, you are vulnerable postpartum. Your usual rock-solid immune system may not kick in, so don't wait to act.

"I convinced myself I had a tumour in my breast. For four days I was in silent hell, thinking I was dying, before I called my mom. She screamed with laughter and told me it was a blocked milk duct and I should just massage it out during the next feed."

> *"I kept thinking I was going to die and that my husband and baby would make up a family without me."*

Remember those days of lying in bed nursing a cold with a DVD and some MedLemon? Over. Remember long mustard baths to ease aching muscles? Finished. Recovery time? No more. The good thing is that you will get on with healing in record time and few complications fall into the category 'long-term'.

Let's look at some of the bodily changes you may experience.

Anxiety and paranoia

> *"I was certain my husband was having an affair while I was at home looking after his baby."*

The rapidly changing state of your body and radical change in your life can lead to all sorts of paranoia and anxiety. If you are worried, check it out with your nurse, but just trust that all sorts of strange things are going to happen and you are probably totally okay. Also see Nightmares (pg 71) and Chapter Eight on depression.

Your obstetrician is your first point of call. The delivery fee covers all complications and visits up to your six-week checkup. If you cannot get hold of him, leave a message with the receptionist or call the emergency number, and he will get back to you. Do not feel he is inaccessible or too busy to bother with what you think is a small complaint. This is the most critical time in caring for you, and he is best placed to advise you on treatment for any complication, from a cold to a serious problem.

Bruised or broken tailbone

This can be incredibly painful and can be a result of a narrow pelvis or the baby moving down in an unusual position. Prepare yourself for the possibility of a long recovery, as there is nothing you can do to speed up the healing of this impossible-to-set bone.

Get pain relief from your doctor.

This is one injury to take lying down. Don't sit on your tailbone. Either lie on your side or get a sitting ring. Heat takes the pain away temporarily, but you want to ice the area rather, to reduce swelling.

" I wanted to have people around me constantly otherwise I would drive myself mad with dreadful thoughts. "

Back pain

Some women experience severe back pain after the birth. Others experience immediate relief from pain they had in pregnancy.

The back pain could just be bruising and sore muscles from a long and difficult labour. A mustard bath, arnica back rub or hot-water bottle can bring relief.

It could also be a posture strain from your weakened abdominal muscles. This will persist until you rebuild those muscles. If you had a vaginal delivery, start doing stomach exercises immediately.

Pay attention to breastfeeding techniques. Make sure you are not slouching to get your baby into position. Rather stick to lying down if you are placing pressure on your back.

Hours of holding three or four kilos can put strain on your back. Watch your movements to make sure you are not under strain.

Bruised eyes

Looking a bit like Benicio Del Toro? This is a direct result of labour. It's caused by the strain of pushing during the second phase. The tiny capillaries in your eyes can rupture causing bloodshot eyes. Black eyes are the result of the capillaries under your eyes rupturing. Both will heal within two weeks, but you are not going to look your glowing best in the photos. Ice packs, tea bags or a hunk of cold meat will reduce swelling. Arnica helps with bruise recovery.

Bigger feet

Not fitting back into your Nine West kitten-heels?

Swelling of the feet is partly due to water retention, partly due to a loosening of ligaments in your body and that includes the ones that hold your foot bones together. The swelling due to water retention will go down within a month of birth, but the bad news is those ligaments are not going to pull the bones back into place. The even worse news is – your feet can get bigger with every pregnancy.

See Swelling (pg 78) for treatment tips.

Carpal tunnel syndrome

This feels a bit like your hand is mildly paralysed and you can have pain in the ligaments that sit on the inside of your wrist.

If this develops soon after the birth, it is directly related to water retention. Your wrist ligaments are enveloped in water and this area can become swollen along with the rest of your extremities. This puts pressure on the nerves that control your hand.

- Immobilise your wrist whenever you can with a splint from a physio.
- Reduce water retention by keeping hydrated. See other tips under Swelling (pg 78).
- Take fast-absorbing magnesium before bed.
- Supplement with twenty-five milligrams to fifty milligrams a day of Vitamin B complex.

As your baby grows, your hand ligaments take strain, with the weight of picking her up continually. This will be exacerbated if you tend to favour one arm.

Practise using the other arm, until it gains strength and you can carry your child with equal dexterity with either arm.

Give your hands a break. Stop using your hands and pick your baby up using your entire arm.

Yoga works on balancing the body, which is what you need to overcome a one-side weakness.

Rub arnica cream or gel into the ligament and manually massage it to increase blood flow to the area.

Cracked nipples

Imagine a paper cut on your nipple. That's what cracked nipples feel like. The good news is they heal fast. They can arrive at any point and are not restricted to the first few months. In fact, as the sucking mechanism grows stronger, the likelihood of this complication developing increases. The most natural remedy is to run your own breast milk over your nipples. Calendula cream

> **TIP**
> Don't lock the bathroom door in the first few weeks. No matter how badly you don't want any accidental walk-ins when you are crouching in the nick, you are still in recovery. You don't want to pass out and not be able to get help.

also hastens healing. Try honey, rosewater or almond oil or commercial lanolin preparations. Remember to wash these remedies off before feeding.

Quite a few beauty salons offer laser treatments on your nipples. These are effective and a few sessions of a low-grade laser will stimulate the regeneration of your skin cells and promote healing.

Constipation

This can cause very unfunny discomfort if left for too long.

Get moving:

- Don't wait to act. The longer you wait, the bigger the stool. You can kick-start the process with a stool softener or a mild laxative. Check with the pharmacy.
- Once you have had a movement, keep a close eye on things. Remember that prevention is better than cure.
- Move fast onto a longer-term prevention of constipation by increasing fresh fruit and fibre in your diet and staying away from refined wheat products. You need to get to a point where you are not using drugs to go to the loo.
- Drink lots of water and add linseeds to your salads and cereal.
- Exercise will also get things moving.

" There is still nothing to beat Black Forest tea to ensure a morning movement. "

" I was so paranoid about going to the loo, I ate only fruit for the first two weeks. My sister had suffered chronic constipation after her birth and had put the fear of God into me. "

" I massaged my belly daily to reduce constipation. Use grapefruit, lavender and patchouli oils and massage your intestines in a clockwise motion. This is the same action you use on your baby to aid digestion. "

> *My mother gave me a bottle of cod-liver oil. I didn't know you could still buy that stuff. I drank the whole thing, before reading the recommended dosage of one tablespoon. It worked within two hours.*

- If you have had a C-section, your bowels will be particularly sluggish, as they are slow to come round from the analgesic. It's prudent not to move on to solids until you have passed at least two bowel movements.

> *Nothing gets my system working better than a double espresso and a cigarette.*

Engorgement

There is a difference between having full breasts and engorged breasts. It's like Marilyn Monroe vs Pamela Anderson.

Breastfeeding consultants say there is no need to ever get engorged. That may be true if you never leave the house and have milk on tap.

Engorged breasts are painful, the skin is taut and fragile, your nipples feel tight and your entire breast aches. This is a familiar place for all breastfeeding moms. Any change in the routine or the baby's continual growth spurts will lead to engorgement. The most important thing is to deflate those mammas.

> *I find champagne will stimulate my milk production. The next day, I will have to contend with leaking breasts at work they are so engorged.*

> *I knew by 11.45am that I could not go a moment longer without release and I raced home. There was my nanny wiping my daughter's mouth. She had just finished a full bottle. No. No. No. I tried to force my nipple in, but she would have none of it. Oh hell, the pain. Upstairs, into shower, hand milking both breasts. Little relief. In went cabbage leaves, suit back on, back in car crying with frustration and pain. All in a day's work for a mom. Bloody hell.*

UNDER PRESSURE:

- Nurse frequently, express or manually milk your breasts.
- If you recognise engorgement early enough, slap those cold cabbage leaves in your bra.
- Pay particular attention to moving any lumps down, towards the nipple and out while nursing or expressing.
- You can also try mixing the juice of marigold leaves with vinegar and dipping your breasts into it.
- Try a damp cloth steeped in cool water containing a few drops of lavender or fennel oil.
- Remember that applying heat may make you feel temporarily better, but it will exacerbate swelling.

"My breasts were leaking so badly during a conference that I had to send my assistant to the pharmacy to buy some breast pads. She came back with sanitary towels. I gave my presentation with two pads stuck down my bra. My jacket was fully buttoned in the midsummer heat."

"Despite reading countless books, I was taken by surprise by the ferocity of my milk coming in. I woke in the night with a lump the size of a tennis ball in my right breast. I had no idea what it was. At a loss, my husband called my mother. She came over at 4am, got me in the bath face down and butt in the air and supervised me, manually milking my breasts, while my husband looked on with the occasional word of encouragement. It was not a high-point."

Episiotomy scar

An episiotomy is a medical intervention by an obstetrician or midwife with a pair of scissors, while a tear is a natural process. The damage can range from a small nick to a rip-roaring tear that goes from vagina to rectum.

" The pain from my episiotomy healing far outstripped the pain of the labour and birth combined. "

THERE ARE FOUR DEGREES OF TEARING

1. Your skin will tear.
2. The skin and perineal muscle will rupture.
3. Your skin, perineal muscle and anal sphincter (this is the muscle that controls your wind and bowel movements) all tear.
4. All of the above tear, plus your rectal mucosa. This is the skin around your bowel.

Any injury of third or fourth degrees will be stitched under an anaesthetic by an obstetrician.

It is not a big procedure but is absolutely critical as the

" My husband witnessed my episiotomy and was incredibly traumatised by the process. He wanted so sue the gynae who performed it and has refused to speak to him since. It has made the process uncomfortable for me; I just want to get on with my life. "

" I came through childbirth unscathed, but to this day, fifteen years later, I still have pain from my episiotomy scar. I still feel angry at my gynae for cutting me so deeply, although he gave me all the reasons in the world. "

success of your stitching will be what prevents you having fecal incontinence through damage to the muscles controlling your bowels. Most South African obstetricians cut in the European style by making a J-shaped cut at a 45-degree angle (mediolateral) towards your leg, whereas US-style is a cut heading downwards towards your bum. The former heals with more pain, but the latter has a greater risk of tearing further into a third or fourth degree wound.

It is going to be itchy and sore as hell as the skin heals. Healing should take six weeks in theory, but some women report pain from their scar for up to two years. The perineum is also the seat of your base chakra, the center-point of your sexual organs and a hugely emotional part of the body. Don't underestimate the vulnerability you feel around this area.

AVOID INFECTION

You don't want to even think about it getting infected.

- Clean every few hours, with cotton wool dipped in a diluted antiseptic solution like Savlon or Dettol. If this is too painful, use a little squirt bottle or bidet.
- Dip your tail in regular sitz (salt water) baths once you get the go-ahead from your doctor.
- Always wipe and wash from front to back.
- Keep the stitches dry. First prize would be to walk around bottomless, not easy with postpartum bleeding. Dry them with a hairdryer.

REDUCE THE PAIN

- Get an ice pack on the area, as soon as possible, to reduce or minimise swelling.
- Keep off your butt.

- Pour tepid water between your legs as you pee. This will dilute the urine and minimise the stinging. If even this is painful, pee while you are in the bath. Relax, it's totally hygienic. You can also use the bidet.
- Ask about localised antiseptic creams, iodine creams or painkillers.
- Don't get constipated. Drink lots of water and take a laxative or stool softener if needed to get your through the early days.

If you had a third or fourth degree wound you will be advised to have a C-section for your next birth, as you run a significant risk of developing fecal incontinence should you deliver with the scar.

Fecal incontinence

The bottom line? Fecal incontinence means you'll have trouble controlling bowel movements, or gas, for some time after the birth. It's not common at all and usually only seen in women who have had a forceps delivery or a fourth degree tear that cuts into the anal sphincter. It's a low blow, but you will get the control back in a few months with some work. Severity will range from needing a nappy to uncontrollable farts. It's a good reason to stay at home.

It can also be caused by a rectal prolapse. This requires a longer-term treatment. See Prolapse bulge on pg 73.

" It took me three months to regain control of my bowel sphincter. I did not have to wear a pad for it, but when I needed to go I had to run. "

" I did 400 Kegel exercises a day; I was so determined to get rid of the incontinence. It was under control within four weeks and my husband was none the wiser. "

" I walked around with a soft gel icepack in my pants for a few days. It really helped reduce the swelling. "

TIP

Kegels bring oxygenated blood to the area and boost healing.

Get cracking with those Kegel exercises, fast.

Consult a specialist physio to help you work on those muscles.

Fever

Any temperature of 38°C/100.4°F or above or any flu-like symptoms, should be reported immediately to your doctor. This is the first indication of an infection. Any infection of the placental site, bladder, stitches or breasts needs to be dealt with swiftly with antibiotics. You can get milk fever on the third or fourth day. This will feel like a low-grade cold with a slight rise in body temperature but will only last around twenty-four hours.

Hair loss

This will kick in from month three, and it can fall out in clumps or just slowly move from your head on to your brush. It's due to another hormonal change from pregnancy, when hair should be thick and radiant, to post-pregnancy. Hair loss should diminish by month six and return to normal by month twelve. Relax. You are not going to end up looking like Bruce Willis. But if your hair is looking ratty and dreadful, consider going short and chic for a while.

Hearing loss

This is extremely rare and little is known about it. It is usually temporary, but you need to consult an ear, nose and throat specialist as well as an ontologist (hearing specialist).

Haemorrhoids

Haemorrhoids, more fondly referred to as piles, are varicose veins in your rear. They are generally quite itchy and often painful. Sometimes you won't feel them at all, and their discovery will be an unpleasant shock. Don't think they always look like a bunch of grapes dangling from your bot; they can actually be only the size of a single raisin and remain neatly tucked away. Piles are common both during and after pregnancy. They work the same way as varicose veins do in your legs. They are essentially veins swollen with blood because they are battling to pump the blood back up your body because of the pressure of your uterus on that area. A lot of pressure in that region like a big push during childbirth or even constipation will exacerbate the swelling.

Hygiene is critical – keep the area clean with regular sitz baths and thorough wiping after bowel movements.

Use a plastic squirt bottle if it's too sensitive to touch.

Witch hazel compresses can give relief.

Kegel exercises will help the area recover.

Consult a doctor or pharmacist for a haemorrhoid ointment like Preparation H, to reduce vein swelling and give topical relief.

TIP

Try and slip the veins back inside your bum so they are not rubbing against your legs and skin. They are sensitive to the touch, but just take a deep breath, smear your finger with Preparation H and push them back in gently.

Postpartum haemorrhage

PPH is the most widely recognised definition of blood loss after birth in excess of half a litre (two cups) for a natural vaginal birth and one litre for a Caesarean-section birth.

Most haemorrhages happen within twenty-four hours after birth and will be handled by medical staff. The most common cause is uterine atony, which is when your uterus fails to contract properly after the child is born.

Hospitals routinely administer the hormones oxytocin, pitocin, methergine or hemabate as an injection within a minute of delivery to ensure the uterus contracts rapidly to deliver the placenta. A significant blood loss will be treated with a transfusion. Bleeding that cannot be controlled using drugs often requires surgery, including hysterectomy, which entails the removal of the uterus.

Fairly heaving bleeding is normal after childbirth. But it should

" I left my wife, as I took our new baby to a room along with the paediatrician, so they could gather stem cells. When I walked back into the room, my wife was lying in a bath of blood. Her entire body was convulsing with shock. Her eyes never left mine as the doctors worked to stop the bleeding. The shock and trauma of that totally overshadowed all the joy of my new baby for weeks. I thought she was dying. "

" Six days after my delivery, I walked five minutes up to the shops. When I arrived the shop assistant rushed over to tell me I had "spilled on my pants". It was a spreading stain of blood. Rather than ask for help, I walked home. By the time I got there, the blood loss was severe. I thought I was dying. My mother lifted me into the car, ordered me to hold my baby and we rushed to an emergency room. I was literally sitting in a deep pool of blood and my heart was racing uncontrollably. Mom was talking calmly to me the whole way. I had lost close on six litres of blood and was given an immediate transfusion. "

start tailing off after four days. If the blood flow is consistently heavy, shows no signs of stopping, or if you start passing large clots (larger than an apricot), let your caregiver know.

IN THE EVENT OF HAEMORRHAGE:

1. Call an ambulance.
2. Lie on the floor and elevate your legs.
3. Massage your uterus in a downward motion. Use medium to heavy pressure. This will be severely uncomfortable, bordering on painful. Use breathing techniques to relax and flow with the pain, also make sure you do not tense up your abdominal muscles.

Infection

Postpartum infections are more common than you think. Your body is debilitated and opportunistic bacteria can attack quickly. You are more at risk if you had a long and difficult labour ending in a C-section or had internal fetal monitoring.

Topping the list is endometritis – an infection of the lining of your uterus. Your cervix, perineum, vagina and vulva are all susceptible to infection.

Bear in mind, any wound has the potential to get infected – including your C-section or episiotomy scar.

The most common symptom of infection is fever. Other symptoms include a smelly vaginal discharge and lower abdominal or localised pain. Scar infections may have redness and swelling around the scar or a discharge. Any infection will be treated with antibiotics.

" My blood loss was so severe I couldn't walk for the first four days I was home. I crawled around the house and up and down our stairs. I pushed myself so hard. I just couldn't relax and let people look after me. "

" I ended up in the ER, six days after my birth, with a severe bladder infection. The doctor suspected I had picked it up from the birthing pool at the hospital. I would dread every trip to the toilet, knowing I was facing crippling pain. I told no one and refused all visitors, I was so determined just to get it over with and get home with my baby. "

> **"** It was only a few days after the birth that my obstetrician inquired gingerly about my labia. He then told me that during the birth, it had blown up to the size of a balloon, from the pressure. It had split and required three stitches. He looked at it and deemed it healing perfectly. But the imagery alone had traumatised me. I was unsure as to what I had left 'down there', and far too scared to look. It was about three weeks later, my hand trembling, that I angled a make-up mirror and looked. One labia lip was blue-black with a bruise. It was an unpleasant shock. I did not want to look further and I did not allow my husband's eyes near me for over four months. He could touch, but not look. **"**

Labia

> **"** I have an extra fold on my labia since the birth. My lips are more 'outdoors' than they used to be. **"**

It's a bit of a surprise to learn your labia have swollen to the size of a tennis ball during the birth. This tissue is traumatised and can swell massively as the baby descends. Treatment is the same as a sore perineum: get ice packs on fast to reduce swelling followed by sitz baths.

Mastitis

This breast infection will hit one in twenty women and a fair share of cows.

It's caused by germs that often pass to you from your baby, through cracks in the nipple. It is opportunistic as nursing moms are often run down and susceptible to infection. Other causes are: failing to remedy engorgement or having a blocked duct that has become infected.

> **"** I felt like a red-hot needle was pushed through my nipple every time my baby suckled. The pain took my breath away. **"**

You will feel like you have the flu and your infected breast will hurt like hell. It will be engorged, red, swollen, throbbing and hot.

" I could feel every heartbeat through the taut veins in my breast and right up into my armpit. Feeding was excruciating pain. I lay in a hot bath for two hours desperately trying to take the edge off, before I eventually called my doctor's emergency number. The healing process took longer than I had imagined and it was a constant pain until it healed, ten days later. "

What is important is that you catch it early and get treatment.

- Whatever you do, don't stop feeding. It is critical that your breasts are regularly emptied to take the edge off the pain. If suckling is too painful use a breast pump or manually express. This is a painful and emotionally draining time.
- The antibiotics will kick in within forty-eight hours and start to clear the infection. Just get support, stay in bed and know that it will pass.
- Heat on your breast will help the letdown reflex and take the edge off the pain for a while.
- Take garlic capsules or try witch hazel, applied directly to the sore spot.
- Look under Engorgement (pg 61) for other remedies.
- Don't ignore this. If untreated, it can lead to breast abscesses, which require antibiotics and surgery.

Nightmares and dark imaginings

Either during sleep or during a fit of anxiety, nightmarish visions and imaginings about your new baby are totally normal. These can range from mild anxiety over its safety to gruesome and disturbing images of dreadful scenarios. New parents can become consumed with worry over the wellbeing of their newborn baby

" I kept thinking of horrific scenarios in everyday household moments. Like I would trip while walking down the stairs and drop my baby. "

and sometimes, those thoughts become intrusive and debilitating, causing some parents to require psychiatric care in a condition known as postpartum psychosis.

Homeopathy: Hypericum.

Post-natal depression

Most women experience the 'baby blues', but about twenty per cent of new moms experience depression. Post-natal depression is discussed in detail in Chapter 8.

" *I was stark-naked, mid-winter, in the garden, clawing at the ground, trying to dig myself into the ground. I was keening like a wolf, as my family looked on in horror. After three weeks of rising paranoia and mania, I had hit a point of no return. I knew I needed help. My husband took me to the clinic that night. I was removed from my baby and under observation for three weeks before I could face returning. It put a huge strain on my family and support system, but it saved my life.* "

" *I kept imagining someone would come through the door to tell me my baby had just stopped breathing. I tried to imagine how I would react and what I would do. I planned everything, down to the last detail of the funeral, in my head.* "

Pigmentation marks

The dark pigmentation marks (chloasma) on your face or belly were caused by hormonal changes during pregnancy that resulted in an overproduction of the skin pigment melanin.

As your hormones return to normal levels, the marks may fade gradually but often don't.

Exposure to the sun can actually cause them to darken further.

Products with fruit acids that remove the protective top layer of your skin can exacerbate pigmentation after exposure to the sun.

Contraceptives that contain oestrogen and progesterone are thought to cause chloasma, so be aware of that additional factor.

If the patches don't lighten within a year, you can consider using a bleaching cream. Take advice from your dermatologist or beautician, rather than buy an over-the-counter cream solution. You could also consider a laser peel.

Prolapse bulge

So you've noticed a bulge or feel that something is not right down there?

Your entire vaginal area is made up by a series of organs (uterus, bladder, bowel, vagina) held in place by muscles. Pregnancy and

" I was told by my gynae, ten months after my baby's birth, that my uterus had dropped, and I would have to consider a hysterectomy. I was twenty-eight at the time and was devastated by the news. I went for a second opinion and was told that a few sessions with a physio should sort me out. I simply exercise regularly and work on my pelvic floor and I have reversed the damage. "

childbirth can place these supporting muscles under strain and a shift in their level of support can mean one of these organs is no longer held as tightly in its place.

This does not always mean there is anything wrong with any of these organs; they are simply sitting in a different place.

BLADDER

Name: Cystocele or urethrocele.

Touch: A bulge or new contour in the top wall of your vagina or externally.

Means: Weakened muscles mean your bladder has dropped lower.

Worst case: Bladder is bulging out of your vaginal opening.

Feels: Bladder constantly feels full. Stress incontinence.

RECTUM

Name: Rectocele.

Touch: A bulge in your vaginal passage. You will feel pressure in the rectum if you push it.

Means: You rectum is bulging upward into weakened vaginal wall.

Worst case: Large protrusion in vagina, in which faeces will sit.

Feels: Continual feeling of a full bowel. Feeling of pressure in rectum. Loss of bowel control. Incomplete bowel movements.

" I have had a rectal prolapse for fifteen years and it is like second nature to me now. It is a secret I chose to keep from my husband. It is now part of my body and I have simply learned new ways to handle it after a year of embarrassment and confusion, when I first felt an unusual bulge. I could opt for surgery, but it is so much part of my toilet routine to just press on my bulge, that surgery is not even necessary. "

UTERUS

Name: Uterine prolapse/dropped womb.

Means: The ligaments holding your womb in place have weakened, so the organ now sits lower in your pelvis.

Worst case: Uterus and cervix hang out of vagina.

Feels: Pain during sex, feeling penis is 'too deep'.

CAN THEY FIX IT?

There are a few options.

Start with regular Kegels.

Physio: Consult your obstetrician, who will refer you to a physiotherapist, to work with you on muscular support.

Pessaries: These devices are fitted into your vagina, to provide muscular support to a bulging prolapse. They have been around since childbirth began and have developed from wooden loops to sophisticated silicone and latex designs.

Surgery: Reconstructing pelvic support draws on a variety of surgical methods to support and tighten the surrounding muscles.

Hysterectomy: This has declined in favour as less invasive options grow in efficacy. About fifteen per cent of hysterectomies are for prolapse.

"
I was told after my first child that I had uterine prolapse and I would have to have a hysterectomy. Thirty years and three more children later, I have never had a single symptom of uterine prolapse. "

Stretchmarks

Prevention is better than cure where this is concerned. Any part of your body that significantly changes shape can get these red tear-like marks. They are more prevalent on your belly, thighs and breasts after pregnancy, but overall weight gain can leave them on your bum, arms, torso or legs. Genetics play a role in the elasticity of your skin. Other factors are hydration and age. These factors will also determine the degree to which the stretch marks will fade as your skin moves back into place. Stretchmarks are best treated while they are still red. By the time they fade to white, you have an almost impossible task to reduce them.

- Keep hydrated from the inside – drink lots of water.
- Hydrate your skin externally: there are lots of creams on the market that claim to target stretch marks. Otherwise, use a base carrier oil – jojoba is the best, or try almond or sesame with a drop or two of wheat germ oil. You can pick up sesame or almond at most pharmacies and health shops.
- Antioxidants, such as Vitamin C and E, can help your body's healing ability.
- Localised oestriol creams are available with prescription.
- A tummy tuck can cut them out. For cosmetic surgery options, see Chapter 7.

"I imagined everything was going wrong with me, from haemorrhaging to heart failure. I felt so out of sorts, so not-myself, that I just panicked at the slightest thing."

Sore fanny

If that baby came out the way nature intended, you are dealing with significant tissue trauma, bruising and swelling in this region. Little wonder it's sore. Your vaginal opening is stretched beyond human dignity. It will heal.

FOUR STEPS TO HEALING:

Don't sit down: The area is bruised and swollen and, like an ankle, the first rule is: take the pressure off. Either lie down, stand or do an elegant side-seat position where there is no contact with your bruised punda.

Heat: Remember, as with any bruising, heat will ease the pain but is counterproductive, as it aggravates the swelling and tissue trauma. Use only if desperate.

Ice it: Sit gingerly on a pack of frozen peas or freeze your maxi pads. Cold reduces swelling.

Arnica: Start with the correct dosage soon after the birth and keep going. Remember not to start before the birth; the homeopathic remedy is fast-acting and should not be taken before the birth or any operation.

"My son is four and I still feel pain in my perineal area. I had a fourth degree tear and took eighteen stitches. It took over a year to heal and was incredibly painful. Now my doctor has conceded that I have permanent nerve damage there. I knew it would take a long time to heal, but I did not think it would take such a toll on my self-confidence and our sex life."

TIP

I bought a vibrating Chinese ball. You insert them in your vagina and leave them vibrating for a while. They cause involuntary muscular contractions that toned my muscles in no time. I pop it in overnight once a week.

Stretched vagina

Welcome to the club. After a vaginal birth, there will be significant stretching and relaxing of the pelvic floor muscles. This will vary, depending on the size of your baby and the number of children you have had. There is no reason your vagina cannot return to its previous size with some exercises. With each successive birth, it will be more difficult to get the form back, but muscles have a huge capacity to grow, so keep working them.

Swelling

Water retention during pregnancy and after the birth is normal, but it should start to go down within four days as the oestrogen drops in your body. If there is still significant swelling four weeks after birth, your body is retaining too much water and you need to contact your doctor. If the swelling is only in one leg and is accompanied by pain, you need to contact your doctor urgently as it could be a thrombosis.

I wore my wedding ring the whole way to nine months. The week after the birth, my legs, arms and hands blew up like balloons. I barely noticed until my husband saw my ring was cutting into my finger. I had to have urgent treatment as my kidneys were failing to eliminate the water.

I started swelling immediately post-birth. It got worse and worse over the next three weeks, despite assurances from my doctor that it was normal. I couldn't bend my legs they were so swollen, and my fingers looked like fat sausages. My arms were close to twice their normal size. Eventually, when my blood pressure started rising dangerously, I was taken to the clinic where I was placed on strong diuretics. Five days later, I had been drained of seven kilograms of water.

- Keep well hydrated.
- Elevate your legs to help your body move the water out – it's fighting gravity. Put bricks under the foot of your bed.
- Take a warm bath. Lying in water helps your body move the fluid from your extremities.
- Make a salad or juice using natural diuretics: cucumber, parsley, coriander, dill, asparagus, green peppers or watermelon.
- Brew a tea with dandelion leaves, another natural diuretic.
- Cut back on tea, coffee and alcohol. These will exacerbate dehydration causing your body to hold on to more water.

Sweating

Sweating like a Greek baker? Relax, it's good for you. Your body is shedding around five litres of water in the first few weeks after the birth and it's coming out every which way it can. It is increased when you breastfeed as your metabolism is working faster, which means you will sweat more.

Urinary incontinence

This is remarkably common, but rarely discussed over tea.

TIP

I did 400 Kegel squeezes a day after my doctor warned I might need surgery. I can feel my bladder strengthening.

TIP

I cured my urinary incontinence by taking strong doses of calcium and magnesium. From needing to wee every twenty minutes, I am back to normal in just under a month.

The most common type of incontinence both during and after pregnancy is stress incontinence, which means you will leak urine when your bladder is under stress – like when you sneeze or cough.

The most common underlying cause is weak pelvic muscle tone, a result of childbirth. There is a misconception that it's the birth that causes this, and a C-section will leave you intact. Wrong sister. While birthing a large baby can certainly worsen it, it's the long months of pregnancy that have put pressure on this organ. Things improve once everything starts to move back into place, but your bladder is stretched. It is then that you will notice stress incontinence.

Your risk is higher if you:

- Have two or more pregnancies.
- Birth a big baby.
- Have pelvic prolapse.

The good news is it's usually temporary and treatable. It can last for two months or up to two years. But it's not generally going to clear up on its own. You will need to put in some hard work with Kegel exercises, with at least a hundred a day to start. If that doesn't do the trick, you may be in line for some surgery to correct it. Your obstetrician will be your first port of call and the one to treat you. Rule out a bladder infection by consulting your doctor.

Homeopathy: Causticum, Aloe socotrina and Pulsatilla nigricans are remedies that may be recommended.

Tissue salts: Take silica and calcium fluoride to help strengthen the tissues.

"I am only twenty-eight, but I am incontinent. I feel far too young for this and it's unexpected after a trouble-free birth eighteen months ago. My doctor has recommended surgery, a huge shock after feeling like I was finally on the mend. I just can't face it yet."

Varicose veins

These blue and swollen blood vessels can disappear by themselves after the birth as your blood volume decreases, but the chance is smaller if you are overweight or have a family history of them. They are most commonly visible on the legs but can appear on the labia or vulva. For a full discussion on how they develop and are treated, see pg 147. Speak to your doctor: it is important to discover whether varicose veins are dangerous or point to a more dangerous health or vascular problem, including thrombosis.

- Raise your legs whenever possible.
- Elevate the end of your bed by placing it on bricks.
- Pressure helps, so buy elastic stockings. If the veins are on your vulva, buy some tight granny panties or cycling shorts.
- Avoid constipation.
- Massage the area upwards with lemon and grapefruit oil.
- Include plenty of fresh garlic in your diet.
- Exercise regularly.

Prevention is definitely better than cure and often the only solution is surgical (see Chapter 7).

Weeping

Ten minutes into the *Bold and the Beautiful* and you are heading for the Kleenex? This is normal even if it's not your style. Your body is going through massive hormonal changes, you are emotionally fragile, physically tender, and your entire life has turned upside down. The waterworks will end eventually.

" I learned how to cry after my birth. It came so easily. Now I have to get out of a habit of crying every time I am tired, frustrated or just gatvol. "

" I wept through my entire pregnancy and the first three months after the birth. I still get teary-eyed when I think about my baby and weep every time I watch the birth video. It's so unlike me. I even sat dry-eyed through Braveheart. "

CROTCH COACH

The good Dr Kegel (rhymes with bagel) spent eighteen years as a crotch scholar, studying the mechanisms of the pubococcygeus muscle (pc), better known as your pelvic floor muscle. And he has been richly rewarded by having one of the best-kept secrets between women as his namesake. If you have gone through your entire pregnancy without doing a Kegel exercise, you have done yourself a major disservice. But we are here to fix that.

FIND THE MUSCLE:

The pelvic floor muscles are attached to the pelvic bone and act like a hammock, holding in your pelvic organs and your urethra, bladder, uterus and rectum. The muscle actually holds all your internal organs in your body.
The easiest way to find these is to stop a flow of urine.
Stop and restart the flow a few times until you get the hang of isolating the muscle without tensing your inner thighs or buttocks.
Another way is to insert a finger into your vagina and tense it around your finger. You'll feel it when you get the right muscles working.

WORK THE MUSCLE:

Tighten and relax the muscle with increasing repetitions. Start with around three sets of ten, and work up to a 100 a day. It's a muscle, so as it starts to grow, you need to challenge yourself by tightening harder or holding longer. It will take eight to ten weeks to even start seeing results, so don't stop.

VARY YOUR KEGELS:

Elevator Kegels: Here you tighten slowly like an elevator going up seven floors. With each floor you tighten further. And slowly release in seven stages as the 'elevator' descends.

Holding Kegels: Tighten and hold for five seconds before releasing. Increase the time, as you get stronger.

WHAT ARE THE BENEFITS?

Better sex: You can give him all sorts of new sensations during sex by tightening those muscles at strategic intervals. They spasm involuntarily when you orgasm.

Less tearing: A well-conditioned muscle is less likely to tear.

It can prevent prolapse of your pelvic organs.

It can help prevent leaking urine when you sneeze or cough. We like that.

NOT FOR BEGINNERS:

There are a number of physiotherapists who specialise in treating the pelvic floor and will administer the below treatments in their rooms. Ask your obstetrician for names.

Vaginal cones: These objects are weighted, tampon-sized devices that you insert and hold in place as you go about your day. Sounds easy? Think again. You are going to have to squeeze your muscles to hold this cone in place. Once you master, it you move onto the next, heavier cone.

Electrical stimulation: This is a probe that stimulates your muscles, forcing them to contract. You can either have it done under medical supervision or buy a home-use unit. Sex shops market another type of device – they call them Chinese, or vibrating, balls. Much more fun.

GOING BUST:

SAYING GOODBYE TO YOUR TUMMY AND BOOBS

It was cruel of Sarah Jessica Parker to flash her taut and toned abs three months after the birth of her son. But also stupid, as we now know she is an alien. A lot of New Yorkers are, but they don't all step out twelve weeks after giving birth with a six-pack and stilettos. So absurd was her feat that Time *magazine picked up on it, pointing out that she had confessed that her twelve week shrink was a standard 'too high for most women'. Not too high for Catherine Zeta-Jones who dropped close to thirty kilos in the same time to look good for her wedding to Michael D. Zeta-Jones and Parker are the public frontrunners in a long line of celebrity moms who seem to think that the physical changes of motherhood are aberrations that need to be erased in record time.*

Elizabeth Hurley, after the birth of her son, made short work of showing the world that there is also sex after childbirth, a fact most women doubt. She was all over the mags looking lush and satisfied hanging off the arm of love maestro Arun Nayar. Are they for real?

CHAPTER 4

Kate Hudson put on thirty kilograms while pregnant with Ryder and women everywhere sighed with relief. "I got huge!" said the former size 28. Four months on she is back down to a size 30 and says she regained her figure by working out two or three times a day. Who does that? Who works out three times a day? Let's give the last word to the woman who makes all real women cringe: Liz Hurley. "I have killed myself to shed the pounds." Dare we even mention the stick-thin Vicky Beckham? No, that would be too much to bear.

"You can get your stomach back, but few women are prepared to put the time in to get the results. I do at least 200 sit-ups every day – and have for the last ten years."

Patricia Heaton is honest. She is the wife in sitcom *Everybody Loves Raymond* and has written a book: *Motherhood and Hollywood: How to Get a Job Like Mine*. She's open about having had plastic surgery, including a tummy tuck and a breast lift." Pregnancies and nursing do something to your body that no amount of sit-ups and working out can fix.

"A lot of people out there who look at magazines, pictures and award shows see all these actresses who have kids and yet look fantastic.

"I love my new boobs. My nipples changed shape from nursing and they look permanently aroused – it's damn sexy."

"I think people really should know that if you also had a team of experts working you for three or four hours a day and you had been fasting for ten days before that and people were lending you $10 000 dresses and $50 000 necklaces, you could look fabulous too."

"He would not latch. Of course I did not know this until I went for the six-week check up and found he was bordering on starvation. The incredible guilt I felt combined with the terrible shock that I had literally starved my own son, was more than I could bear."

Wrapped up

The Chinese wrap four metres of cloth tightly around their torsos to bring down their stomachs, as do many African tribes. Binding the stomach is a common practice and many women swear it's the only way to stave off the pouch, even ex-New Yorker Gwyneth Paltrow confessed to a new-age version of binding to help her stomach shrink back to its tiny self after Apple. It involves living in a pair of reinforced leggings, somewhat like cycling shorts, that squeeze all your bits in ultra-snug. They are hell getting into, but worth the sweat.

But helping your uterus to shrink through binding does not equal a return to flat. It takes far harder work than that. Think of it like this. You take a small balloon and blow it up into the size of a Pilates ball. Then you let the air out. Is it going to shrink? Surely.

Will it ever go back to its original snappy little size? Not unless you are prepared to work on that stomach like your life depends on it. Madonna did it at forty-two which means it's physically possible. Now the rest of us just have to get our heads (if not our tummies) around that.

" I look fantastic in clothes, but put me on a beach and I will want to die. My stomach is like soft dough. "

" There is only one word to hang on to any lift; Wonderbra. "

" My waist slowly returned, but after two kids, my floating ribs just never quite went back to size. "

" I need to switch off my functioning, creative and questioning mind on the endless days of growth spurts when my daughter feeds every hour. I must become a calm and serene mother, lest I remember who I used to be. "

" My mom told me to wrap my torso in cling wrap every day to sweat it back to size. I don't think it worked, but I would have tried anything. "

"The worst scenario is if you have small boobs they blow up. Then when they go you are left with saggy and stretchy sacks, but no boobs."

I still look pregnant

It is a surprise how slowly your tummy shrinks and at your six-week check-up, you look seven months pregnant. Worse, your stomach is no longer a hard ball; it's a soft and squishy mass.

The reason is that it takes time for your body to recover completely from a long pregnancy and a delivery. With the start of labour your uterus will begin to shrink and by week six it should be sitting back in your pelvis. Over the same time your body will start to shed the water it was retaining in all its cells. This will also help your stomach shrink. But these facts don't mean your stomach has gone down totally. You are going to have fat on your stomach, laid down for breastfeeding and that will take some time to work its way off and your abdominal muscles and skin are stretched beyond all imagination.

"Oh heavens I used to have magnificent breasts. I miss them, my husband misses them ... but they are no more."

Will it ever look the same again?

More than just stretching, your skin has actually ruptured many of its elastic fibres during pregnancy, which means your abdominal walls remain soft and flabby after childbirth. Remember that skin is elastic and has a huge capacity to stretch and return to form. Again, your ability to get your stomach's shape back is informed by both genetics and age.

"When my son was three, my husband sat me down and told me I had to stop breastfeeding. It was enough and he wanted his wife back. I knew it in my heart, but I had just battled to let go."

You are looking at around nine months for your skin to shrink back. There are women who have flat stomachs weeks after delivery but they are incredibly rare. Many women report that even if the rest of their body gets back to shape, they still have a fatty pouch on their bellies for years.

Some women say the only part of their bodies that never quite went back to the pre-pregnancy state was their stomachs. Few people naturally have ironing-board stomachs in any case. Ask those girls at the gym with six-packs and they will tell you they do hundreds of sit-ups a day. Don't think your stomach is magically going to shrink like you are a human elastic band. You are going to have to work on it. Exercise helps to speed recovery of abdominal walls. In fact it does more than that – it actually trains your stretched muscles to move back into shape. It's no coincidence that every book tells you to get on the floor as soon as you can and start to gently work your abdominal muscles. You are not aiming for flat at this early stage, you are actually trying to shorten those very stretched muscles so they start to move back into place. If you have had a C-section that went through abdominal muscles, you need to check in with your obstetrician before you start any exercise, but otherwise you need to start seated squeezes and then work towards crunches posthaste.

Squeeze: Sit in a chair or comfortable position with your back ever so slightly rounded. Nothing will move except your abdominal muscles and anyone watching you will see no movement.

Contract your abdominal muscles in a slow squeeze. Pull the lower abs upwards and the upper abs towards your spine. Breathe out as you contract. Squeeze as tight as you can and towards your spine and hold for five seconds before releasing. Repeat ten times breathing out as you contract, in as you release. This controlled squeeze is incredibly effective in toning your abs even when you move on to floor exercises and more vigorous stomach crunches.

" My grandmother bound my stomach with a traditional Xhosa wrap every morning. I wore it for four months until my shape went down. "

" I will bet you any woman with pert breasts has either not had children, or has silicone boosting them up there. "

" I could not bear it. The act of breastfeeding triggered an incredible insecurity in me. I battled on for months in misery before I stopped, and my life started. "

Crunch: This is a more conventional toning exercise. Get on the floor and bend your legs (you can elevate them on a bed or couch). Contract your abdominal muscles to support your lower back. With your muscles contracted, raise your head twenty to thirty centimetres off the ground and lower. Breathe in. Breathe out, contract and repeat. Start with sets of ten, working up to 100 to 200 crunches a day.

Unless you are prepared to work long and hard at rebuilding your abdominal muscles, you will not get rid of your pouch. Don't forget, they have been stretched further than your partner's patience for at least five months, and they are going to need serious work to rebuild.

What about marks?

Getting stretchmarks is bad luck and is mostly genetic. According to the tabloids, Cindy Crawford was desperate to avoid them and tried every cream imaginable to stave them off.

CHEAT A TAUT TUM

- Control top tights are your best-kept secret.
- A wide belt does wonders in creating a waist.
- Hold your stomach in.
- Don't wear clothes with tight waists; they will accentuate your stomach.
- Mix 'n match: Combine Kegels with stomach crunches or squeezes with inner thigh squeezes to save time.

SKIN DEEP

There are shelves of creams and oils at pharmacies and supermarkets that claim to be particularly effective in diminishing the redness of stretchmarks. By all means, give them a try, but don't expect miracle results.

Prescription treatment: Retin-A creams, a vitamin A derivative, show some results as they increase collagen production and actually thicken your skin. These are more effective when used early, and their effect will be reduced with older stretchmarks. But be warned, you cannot use them during pregnancy, only after you stop nursing.

Salon stuff: Some women report the Endermologie machine shows results as the combination of suction and low frequency is supposed to stimulate blood flow to the area and support regeneration.

Eat right: Choose foods high in vitamins C and E, zinc and silica (which helps to form collagen).

Herbs: Homeopaths will recommend creams or oils containing horsetail, ivy, centella and comfrey.

Surgery: Laser surgery is popular in treating stretchmarks, but this will not remove them; it will simply fade the redness of the lines. Abdominal surgery (the tummy tuck) is extremely effective in removing stretchmarks and is an expensive last resort for women who feel their stomachs are scarred beyond all recognition. See Chapter 7 for more details.

Prevention (as far as this is possible) is the best method as once you have a stretchmark it's yours for life. Stretchmarks are actually little scars caused by the excessive stretching of skin and will never disappear totally. It can take several months for the redness of stretchmarks to lighten and a year or more before they turn white and shiny, which is as good as it gets.

Many women also have a dark line down their abdomen called a linea negra. The dark colour will gradually fade over the course of a year, but that too, may never completely go away.

What a boob

Breasts are made to make milk. There are lots of lovely diversions along the way, but their basic biology is powerful and inescapable. They do it efficiently, spontaneously and under a remote guidance system that seems to be out of control most of the time. But it does not mean that breastfeeding is a natural occupation. It's a topic almost as divisive and fraught with emotion as the Middle East. It requires supreme focus, commitment and an extraordinary amount of time. It robs you of your freedom, it can delay your weight loss and it can be emotionally and physically draining. There are some joys no mother will escape: waking up in a bed awash with breast milk, leaking through a breast pad, the grate of a tooth across your nipple, tender breasts, lumps and frustrating hours on an expressing machine that could have been loaned from your local dairy. These machines need to suck your nipple right in so it's around the length of a cow's teat before they can get an ounce. It can be dehumanising, incredibly hilarious and excruciatingly embarrassing.

On a psychological level, breastfeeding can bring on levels of extreme anxiety and inadequacy – particularly if things go wrong, which they frequently do with mastitis, inverted or cracked nipples, lumps and infections.

But nursing is also glorious, poignant and unbearably beautiful. It is all of these things and the sheer commitment of nursing a baby, for however long you choose, is a task that will give you all the rewards it deserves.

Breasts are the physical metaphor for giving and receiving. In ancient times, they were worshipped and immortalised in art and song. Everything about them symbolised nature's abundance and nurturing qualities, for both babe and man. When you start breastfeeding, your breasts become part of this legacy. You may find that you miss your man-magnets when they become baby canteens, but you need to face up to the fact that your relationship with your breasts has changed.

> " *I feel very insecure about my breasts. They literally hang to my belly button and I wear a bra, even when I sleep as they are so ugly, I want them covered.* "

Let down

At some point in my life, I thought I wanted to be Dolly Parton. I would sit enraptured in front of the telly as she swung from the heavens singing *I'd Like To Teach the World to Sing*. It was in the days before computer graphics, so they either let loose a swarm of butterflies and bluebirds or Dolly was a whiz with hand puppets. Sure I was twelve, but Dolly was the perfect woman for me. I had my turn to be Dolly for a day. I went from a solid B cup to an EE overnight. Everyone agreed that my breasts were truly spectacular, but it only lasted a miserly week before they started a slow but steady deflation that ended about eight months later, when I realised my breasts were there no more. Gone. And in

TIP

Expressing is not a spectator sport and is best kept behind locked doors if you want to retain an iota of dignity and feminine mystique.

their place remained the skin but not the glorious soft fat. In sharp contrast to the rest of my body, I had skinny boobs. Skinny and sad.

All women will have smaller breasts after pregnancy. Those who choose not to breastfeed are not saving themselves this. It is during your pregnancy that your breast tissue changes and swells. Its deflation, whether your baby's lips touch your nipple or not, will leave the cells less plump and your breasts appearing less full.

> " During my third pregnancy, my silicone implants drove me mad with pain as my breasts swelled. I begged the plastic surgeon to remove them. The pain abated by the sixth month, but it remained a low-level ache. "

Plump 'em up

Firm up: Nothing you apply to your skin can affect either your breast shape or size. Regular moisture and good care, just like with your face, can slow down the process of aging and retain elasticity, the loss of which is a key factor in droop.

FACT BOX

The average bust line is 91.2 cm.

The most-purchased bra size is 34B.

The proportions of women's cup sizes breaks down to the following:

A – fifteen per cent

B – forty-four per cent

C – twenty-eight per cent

D – ten per cent

The remaining three per cent are AA, AAA, DD and beyond.

Exercise: Because your breasts are made up mostly of fatty tissue and contain no muscle, exercise alone will not change their size or shape directly. However, by working the largest muscle in the chest, the pectoralis major that runs behind your breast, you can help support the breasts and hold them up higher.

" I did a salon slimming treatment with those electrode machines and manual massage. It cost an arm and leg, but I got a few inches off. "

Fake it: There are lots of products out there to pad your bra, without having to use your hockey socks. Water-filled bras, silicone pads you slip into your bra, gel bras or toupee tape, all work to bolster your breasts. They are not that easy to source. Some good lingerie stores will stock silicone- or water-filled bras or will order them for you. Stuttafords has a large range of specialist lingerie.

Check out www.breastenhancers.co.za (call 0860 CURVES) for a catalogue and list of stockists or order online. The bra will be delivered overnight.

" As well as sit-ups, slowly clench your stomach muscles and hold then release every time you do your Kegels. It tones your stomach incredibly. "

Buy right: A good push-up bra can add at least a cup size and is worth every cent.

TIPS

- There is no better investment than a good bra.
- Do not be tempted to go bra-less while nursing. The added weight of your breasts will put additional strain on your skin.
- Keep your skin well hydrated with moisturises, to prevent stretchmarks.
- Hydrate from within by drinking lots of water.

ANATOMY OF A BREAST

Strange, but true: Breasts are large sweat glands that have evolved to produce milk, instead of sweat.

Lobes and ducts: Our breasts are made up of functional and supportive materials. Both are surrounded by fat. Lobes of glandular tissue produce the milk. Each breast contains milk ducts that lead towards the nipple, which acts as the exit point.

The nipple: This consists of the nipple and aureole. Both are as individual in size and shape as their owners and their colour is due to the pigmentation of the incredibly thin skin that makes them up. At the core of the nipple are the fifteen to twenty-five milk ducts. The aureole has numerous small bumps that are actually sweat and sebaceous glands. Both nipple and aureole have a complex system of tiny muscle fibres that control movement in response to cold, arousal and nursing.

Nerves: Both aureole and nipple have a complex system of nerves, from both the sensory and autonomic systems, concentrated in the small area. The latter controls involuntary functions like sweating and arousal. It could explain why stimulation of the nipple can result in vaginal arousal. Some women even report they can achieve orgasm through their nipples.

Lymph glands: Lymphatic fluid is like a grease that keeps the body running smoothly. Its drainage carries away many unwanted byproducts. When you examine your breasts for lumps, you are not looking for tumours, you are looking for swollen lymph nodes – the first indication of an infection or disease.

my story: Janet

I have always had an ironing board stomach. It used to be the envy of all my friends, all my life. I carried weight on my thighs, but my stomach had a six-pack regardless. After my first baby, it went and after my second, my stomach was soft and flabby. Nothing I did could get this over-hang of skin off, it literally just hung over my jeans. I could grab it in a hand and lift it up. Two years later I was morbidly depressed. None of my old clothes suited me anymore. Hipsters and T-shirts, my clothes of choice, made me look like a Tellytubby. I started wearing jackets most of the time rather than sexy pants. I looked like a librarian. Friends would joke about it.

"Expecting your third?" they would say. Or Dan would say jokingly, in front of friends, that I was challenging him on his beer boep. I was devastated. I felt totally unattractive and out of control. I started to doubt myself about everything. What did I used to look like? How did I dress? I could no longer remember my style or if I had any. And yet, I could not find myself in this new look I had. I was tubby and round and I hated myself.

I started researching plastic surgery. I felt like such a fraud – all of thirty-six and going for the cut. I did not tell a soul. The first surgeon I saw was so dreadful, I cried for days. He made me feel like an inferior cut of meat. But the second was fantastic. He told me all about the risks, what to expect, and how long it would take to recover.

Liposuction would not be effective as it was a mass of skin that needed to be removed, not just a pocket of fat. It was expensive so I held off for four months. But once the seed was planted, I couldn't wait. I told Dan and he was incredibly supportive, but he did let me know he thought it a bit vain. We found the money and I went in for the surgery, incredibly excited. I got my body back. I feel so fantastic. I feel like finally, after six years of looking like a mommy, I am sexy, sassy and myself. I have a scar, but it's a small price to pay for a flat tummy. And I do mean flat. I am back in my hipsters and I have told not a soul except my husband about the surgery.

SWEATING
for the
BODY
BEAUTIFUL

Three months after my baby's birth, I realised the only muscle left toned in my entire body was my uterus. Somewhere in the Woolies change-room, between slipping out of a racy red slip and putting on a pair of pink velour tracksuit pants, I found myself standing in my underwear in multifaceted, infinitely angled misery.

"Give yourself time," my mother cooed from the slender luxury of a size 34 and thirty years of selective amnesia. "It will come off in time."
"How much time?" I asked.
"A year," she offered, turning quickly to examine the spring onions.
I wanted a quantifiable schedule. "How long did it take you?"
"It varied with each of you but a minimum of eighteen months each."

That was back in the days when dieting was not an exact science, I rationalised, after the shock wore off days later. She did not know that carbohydrates are another form of fat. She thought dieting was eating cottage cheese instead of butter on her baked potato. She did not have the options I have today.
"I give myself six months."

CHAPTER 5

THE MIRROR TRAUMA HAD ALSO MADE ME REFLECT ON THE LAST FEW MONTHS. It dawned on me that I had made some fundamental miscalculations in the early days.

Week Two: I had entertained some guests for tea. I had emerged in a sexy spaghetti strap vest and maternity pants. Everyone had said I was looking good.

"I can hardly even tell you had a baby two weeks ago," some smirking guest said. My mother quietly slipped her pashmina over my shoulders saying I mustn't get cold.

Spurred on by all the compliments, I made miscalculation number two later that day.

I defied the laws of physics and managed to squeeze into a pair of my old Levis. I had tried them on two days after the birth and was amazed I could not get them higher than my knees. Now I had them on. It had been so long since I had worn them, I just couldn't wait. I giggled as I lay on the floor and literally tucked handfuls of fat into the waistband.

"Look," I screamed triumphantly, sashaying down the stairs. "I'm back in my jeans."

The look of wide-eyed horror on my husband's face said it all. I mistakenly read it as delight. I didn't realise that the top half of my torso looked like a genie popping out of a teeny bottle.

"Wear them round the house a bit first," he suggested diplomatically, "until you are comfortable going out in public in them."

I took them off about ten minutes later. But only because I could not sit down in them.

The first few months were a series of diet devastations as it slowly dawned on me that this fat was just not coming off. Not that losing weight has ever been particularly easy for me. It's just that I never thought I would fail outright. I hired a personal train-

> "Ten months after the birth, I went for a checkup at my doctor. I was back in my old clothes and feeling good about my weight. I got on the scale to find I was still eight kilograms above my pre-pregnancy weight. I felt so damn sorry for myself, I wept the whole afternoon."

er who measured my body fat at forty per cent. Could almost half my entire body be fat? I ran and ran and pushed more weights than Pink. Nothing. Not a kilogram shifted.

I now have new rules. No scales. No diets. No bikinis.

There will be no beach holiday this year.

Time trials

After the birth, there is some level of expectation that your stomach will vanish almost immediately. Sure, you tell yourself, you'll have to deal with the loose skin slowly moving back into place but the general bulk will be gone.

But it is not just your stomach. The fat is everywhere. Despite nine months of living in outsize clothing, it really does come as a shock. You thought it was your pregnant belly that was stopping you from slipping on your Diesels. But now that that has gone, you still cannot get the waistband higher than your knees. What is all that fat doing there? And why do you have dimples on your inner knees, not just your inner thighs?

There are two issues to contend with:

* First. You are actually fat.
* Second. You have an entirely different body. Your stomach alone does not carry your baby, your whole body does.

Some would say your uncooperative body itself is one of the first signs the physical universe is giving you that nothing in your life will ever be the same again.

Underlying it all, is an overwhelming sense of disappointment and self-judgement. Call it the last hangover of your old life, but some part of you thinks that your body and life will just return to

" Everyone was losing weight breastfeeding, but mine wouldn't budge. I was tempted to stop early but kept going until twelve months. A month after I stopped, the weight slowly started dropping. "

normal after the birth, that it was just a tummy you had created not a whole new body and a whole new life for yourself.

Big momma

What sort of weight are we talking about?

You are going to lose a large amount over the birth and the first two weeks.

The average weight gain during a nine-month pregnancy is eleven to fifteen kilograms. If you are underweight pre-pregnancy, you may be advised to gain more weight, in the region of fourteen to sixteen kilograms. If you are overweight when you fall pregnant, your doctor will advise you to gain less, so you remain in a healthy weight zone. A severely overweight woman should gain as little as six to eight kilos.

These figures are averages. But in reality, weight gain can be anything from four to forty kilos. During the birth, expect to lose 5.6 to 6.3 kg:

Baby:	3 kg
Amniotic fluid:	1 kg
Placenta:	800 gm
Fluid loss:	1.5 kg
Blood loss:	500 gm

This leaves 5.4 to 9.5kg of excess weight.

" *I have always been tiny. I put on a staggering thirty kilograms during my pregnancy five years ago and have lost only fifteen of those kilograms. I lost most of those within the first three months and have battled since then to lose more. I have tried everything, from diet pills to soup diets, but I cannot drop the weight. I still have my size eight clothes hanging in my cupboard alongside my size 14s. I simply cannot let go of what I used to be.* "

The absolute minimum additional weight you are going to have to tackle is five kilograms of fat that your body has laid down for breastfeeding reserves, which means women who don't breastfeed are going to have to work extra hard to lose that extra weight.

Your breasts are probably each carrying one kilo of extra weight.

The loss of muscle, as you became sedentary during pregnancy, combined with fat accumulation, means you are looking at body fat of sixty per cent post-birth and a slow fall back to anything near twenty per cent, which is where a woman should aim.

The first thing to do is relax. It's a lot, but you can lose it. Just not as fast as you would expect. How those kilos crept on is no longer relevant and agonising over what you ate is a waste of time. This is a temporary state, but you are going to have to work to get out of it.

As a rule, give yourself a year to return to your pre-pregnancy weight. (This does not mean you will return to your pre-pregnancy body in that time.)

In fact, it is a very real possibility that you will never have that same body again. That's not to say the new body will be any worse, only different.

" I thought I would be back in my old clothes within days of the birth. Nine months later, and I am still up a size. "

" I have never been a health nut, but the second I had Lulu I wanted to be thin and fit. It was so unlike me. From yoga and the odd walk, I was yearning to pound it out on the treadmill. I kept thinking it was a case of wanting to be what I was not, so I resisted the urge for months. A friend then told me she was training for a half-marathon, and it was all the encouragement I needed. The next morning I hauled out a pair of running shoes and joined her on a four-kilometre run. It was bliss for me. Maybe after the physicality of pregnancy and birth, my body suddenly felt a need to be pushed to some limit again. I can't explain it, but I am now driven to exercise pretty hard almost daily. "

SWEATING *for the* BODY BEAUTIFUL

When can I get cracking?

We can't all afford to charter a chopper to calm our tot like Vicky Beckham. This means the most muscle action you are going to get in the first three months is developing a rocking and burping arm. It looks something like the forearm of the Incredible Hulk, but it's only your right arm. By the time twelve months are over, you will outpace your husband in pull-ups and be able to throw the shot put like an Olympian. That's one body part you can look forward to – Madonna biceps. Of course, that's the only body part that will be toned.

Conventional wisdom says don't start dieting or exercising vigorously before you have your six-week checkup. Your doctor will give you the go-ahead to embark on an exercise boot camp. Of course most of us don't give a toss about conventional wisdom. We want our bodies back.

But while you are in the six-week period, your body is still in a very altered state and it's possibly a good time just to give yourself a break for once in your life. If you exercised throughout your pregnancy and are generally fit, there is no reason not to start some gentle exercises at home. You should start with sit-ups within a few days of delivery if you had a natural birth. In any case, remember that your joints and ligaments will still be relatively loose for three to five months, so don't plunge into strenuous activity. You are not the gym bunny you were a few

"I recall standing naked in front of the mirror at thirty-nine weeks, admiring my toned legs. I went as far as to wear mini-skirts to work. It was only months after the birth that I realised they were far from toned. They were the size of those great slabs of carcass hanging at the butchers. They had just looked small in comparison to my stomach."

months ago, and a strained muscle is going to drive you to distraction. So start with caution and build up. If the last time you exercised was on the high school tennis team, now is not the time to start training for a half-marathon.

Your body will let you know if you are doing too much too soon. If your vaginal bleeding (lochia) gets increasingly red or restarts, chances are you are pushing yourself too hard.

Exercising after a C-section

Early exercise will increase healing capacity. It also assists in over-coming constipation, a major setback for some C-section moms.

- There is no medical reason for you to be bedridden or inactive, and you can even start gentle stomach exercises, unless your abdominal muscles were severed in the operation.
- Start slowly with a walk to the shops and increase as you feel stronger and more able to move further or faster.
- Distinguish between good pain and bad pain. Mild pain may occur as you start to get parts of your body moving that have been inactive. You can push through it, but don't ignore a sharp pain.

"I pushed myself incredibly hard from my six-week checkup. I cut down calories radically and exercised six days a week. I did not lose a single kilogram. I had fifteen kilograms to lose, and I wanted to waste no time. I was running forty-five minutes, three times a week and lifting weights the other three. By month five, I had burned out. I stopped even trying. I stopped breastfeeding at six months and a month later the weight started dropping off me. I was so sick of dieting, I barely noticed. But it came off at about two to three kilograms a month and I am slowly getting back into my clothes."

What's changed about you

1. BREASTFEEDING

Despite the fact that everyone tells you that you will lose your weight breastfeeding, this is rarely true. Some women do drop weight like a stone while nursing. Others cannot shift a gram until months after they stop. Each body is unique and will respond differently to breastfeeding. For a good indication of your body's hormonal reaction to feeding, chat to your mom, sisters or aunts to find out their experiences. Chances are, you are cut from the same cloth.

Can you start to cut down your calorie intake while breastfeeding? Certainly. What a good time to get into a healthy eating pattern, especially if you gained unnecessary weight during your pregnancy.

There is absolutely no risk to your baby. You body is geared to shed its own fat for the good of the baby. It has specifically catered for this event by padding you all over with fat reserves. Let's be sensible. Even in Somalia, nomadic tribes who sometimes eat only once a week manage to raise totally healthy babies. We are bamboozled by misinformation and pushed to eat beyond our needs.

If you are calorie restricting, your baby will be fine. The only risk you run is to yourself. The hormones that are protecting your bones from losing calcium during the pregnancy are no longer active, so you need to monitor your calcium intake.

Also, your own energy reserves can run down fast, leaving you tired and listless if you are under-eating.

Don't do anything stupid like embark on a grapefruit fast. There are a wealth of good, balanced eating programmes out there that are safe to do while breastfeeding. Even a dramatic

"I cut out all wheat and sugar. Over four months, I lost ten kilograms and didn't miss it at all."

calorie reduction (to a healthy level, of course) will not harm your baby in the slightest.

2. PEER GROUP PRESSURE

There is a huge misconception that you have to eat like a marathon runner to breastfeed a baby. In fact, family members can round on you like a pack of dogs should you pass over a second portion of trifle. You continually find yourself pressured into eating more than you ever imagined with the reassurance that you need to 'eat for two'. That is nonsense. In fact, you need only an extra 500 calories a day while nursing – and that's about two extra pieces of fruit. You need to stand your ground if you are eating to make other people feel better. All you need to produce enough milk is extra fluid, preferably water.

3. METABOLISM

Metabolism, simply put, is the rate at which your body burns up and uses the food you eat. The faster and more efficiently the metabolism runs, the more calories are burned by the body for energy and the more weight you will lose. More important is that the calories burned by the metabolism are partly, if not mainly, in the form of body fat. Ayurvedic medicine believes that your *agni* (fire) is all but extinguished after giving birth and needs to be carefully stoked again with warm foods, warm liquids and brisk daily massage. It suggests you avoid any raw or cold foods and even steam your fruit, to warm your body and restore metabolism.

Each of us has a unique basal, or resting, metabolic rate. This is the amount of energy your body would require to function if you just lay in bed all day (a luxury you give up with a baby). Everything your body does to keep itself going requires energy – making new cells, growing hair, pumping blood, feeding organs

" I fasted one day a week, taking in only water. It gave me a sense of control and a renewed vigour. The weight came off slowly. "

and moving around. You are burning calories every second of the day whether you are digesting food, sitting in a chair or sleeping.

In fact, your resting metabolism is responsible for approximately sixty per cent of all calories (energy) used in the body.

- Physical activity accounts for approximately thirty per cent.
- Digesting and processing meals accounts for ten per cent.

This is why metabolism is primarily genetic. The only amount you can really influence is the thirty per cent that accounts for your physical activity component.

This also means any starvation diet, or even skipping meals, will rob you of a portion of the ten per cent you use to digest food. It's a large component so beware of skipping meals.

Your thyroid gland regulates several hormones and it drops production of most of these significantly after birth.

It returns to normal functioning in three stages; the length of these will depend on whether you breastfeed. Breastfeeding usually stimulates the metabolism.

Stage one: Hyperthyroidism is where the thyroid goes into overdrive. This often results in anxiety and insomnia. This stage can last from three to six months.

Stage two: Hypothyroidism is where production is slowed. During this phase you can experience lethargy and weight gain.

Stage three: Output has reached pre-pregnant levels. This will vary depending on whether you breastfeed and can take up to two years.

" *I stopped drinking alcohol to lose weight. It was the start of a healthier lifestyle for me – less excuse to miss gym, less late night pizzas to sober up. Over the twelve months I went from size 38 to 32.* "

METABOLISM AFTER BABY:

TRUE:

- It is genetic.
- Men have faster metabolisms than women because of a higher muscle mass.
- A sedentary pregnancy means you have lost a lot of muscle mass or tone.
- By increasing muscle mass or tone, you can increase your metabolism.
- Crash diets slow down your metabolism.
- Exercise speeds it up a bit as you are using more energy.
- Metabolism has nothing to do with the number of bowel movements you pass in a day or how quickly you get hungry after eating.
- Breastfeeding will use more calories.
- If you have dieted your whole life, the chances are you have almost wiped out your metabolism.
- In case you missed the most important point, we will repeat it: Metabolism is first and foremost genetic.

FALSE:

- Your metabolism is faster or slower at different times of the day. "Not true," say most diet docs. This means a meal you eat at 2pm will be digested and used at the same rate as one eaten at 11pm. Time is not the issue. But eating late at night usually means you are packing away an extra meal or snack a day.
- Cardiovascular exercise will raise your resting metabolism. Nope; it will only raise it (burn more calories) for the duration of the exercise and possibly for a short period after exercising.
- Everyone burns calories at the same rate. Sorry, not true. The leaner you are and the more muscle mass you have, the faster you burn calories.

Five tips to looking lean

1   Let's say it again: get control-top tights.
2. Never wear underwear that is too tight. A fat pocket hanging over your bra strap will appear to add ten kilograms.
3. Move up a dress size. Tight is only sexy when you are toned.
4. Cut out the labels. It's depressing to step into an XL pair of pants. It's a fashion disaster if your label hangs out.
5. Step into a pair of glam stilettos. If you can't make your legs thinner, at least make them look longer.

DON'T DO IT:
Crop tops
Tight pants
Dungarees
Bikinis
Pleated jeans

WARDROBE ESSENTIALS:
A stylish cotton Indian kaftan
Glam accessories
Expensive sunglasses

"After my fourth baby, I never lost the weight. I was always too hungry, too busy, too tired. Any excuse in the world really. There was no epiphany, decision or turning point. One day, I simply started cutting everything I ate by half. I would dish up my normal helping. Then cut everything in half and load it on to another plate. Chocolate cake, toast and Camembert with figs, pizza – it all got the same treatment. I ate the same things, just half the volume. A year later I weighed myself and I was twelve kilograms lighter. It was painless and it has never crept back. I still eat probably half of what I used to and it's still a lot."

Spend on accessories, not on good clothes, until your weight has come down to a level you can deal with.

How long will I be a size 38?

Pregnancy weight loss varies from person to person. If you have a metabolism and waist like Audrey Hepburn, expect to be fitting back into your bikini cut denims in six weeks to two months. If you lean more to the Anna Nicole-Smith type physique, you are in for a far longer wait.

- **Get real.** If you are someone who has always battled with your weight, this will be no exception. The sheer volume may give you initial drive, but you will need lots of willpower to last the race.
- **Know your genes.** Chat to your mom and sisters. How long did it take them? Did they lose while breastfeeding or only when they stopped? You are born with a genetic toolbox that, try as you might, you cannot lock away in a cupboard.
- **Don't over-share.** Your partner really does not want to be asked repeatedly whether you look fat. You do. If you feel the need to talk endlessly about your love handles and bemoan your soft and dimpled body, find a buddy. Men are simple

"
I have had an issue with my weight for as long as I can remember, so the self-loathing I felt when, at eighteen months post-birth, I was still twelve kilograms heavier was a familiar place for me. I felt I was almost justified in throwing in the towel and accepting this new body. I justified it, tried to love it and repositioned myself as a voluptuous woman who embraced her rolls. But I am just fooling myself. Nobody really wants to be fat. "

"After I had Shane, I just rolled into his second, then third year with at least twenty extra kilograms. It became my story, my image and my new look. I was a glamorous, kooky and voluptuous mom. My role as mom defined me, all at the age of twenty-three. I went from modelling in a size 10, to a sexy single mom who wore a size 38. The combination was very appealing to men and I was never short of attention and relationships. But I woke up one night, in the middle of my thirty-eighth year and realised that I lost myself somewhere along the line. The young, gorgeous girl in me was almost gone. I started dieting. I am still dieting. It is the toughest thing I have ever done, and it's going so slowly I want to give up every day. I feel like if it was meant to be, it shouldn't be this tough. But I am keeping going."

creatures. There are only so many times you can point out how bad you look before he starts to believe you.

- **Fake it.** It's dead boring to feel fat and ugly; just imagine how boring it is for everyone else to hear you talk about it. Deep breathe and purr: "I am just *lurving* these sexy curves I've got going. It's such a refreshing change." Men will buy it if it's delivered with self-confidence, you fraud.

Dieting for dummies

"The day I got my period back, eight months after the birth, I felt my body change gear. I knew I was back to normal and felt it was time to start losing the weight."

A lot of what we know about diets comes through word of mouth, advertising or magazine articles. Dieting is an industry that rakes in $33 billion a year in the United States alone.

There is a huge amount of misinformation and misdirection out there, promising quick fixes and painless results. There are just about as many theories on how best to lose weight as there are books on dieting. Starting a diet with the wrong information is about as rewarding as window-shopping.

To the medical profession, the formula for losing weight is very simple. To maintain your current weight, you need to balance the amount of calories you eat with the amount of calories being used by your body. To lose weight, you need either to decrease the number of calories you eat or increase the amount of calories you burn. To lose half a kilogram, you need to decrease your overall intake by 3 500 calories. This means that if you want to lose 450 grams a week, you must decrease what you consume by 500 calories – the equivalent of four apples – a day or increase the calories you use by 500 a day which, depending on your size, is around a ninety-minute walk a day or a 45-minute jog.

For most people, combining both strategies is the easiest way to reach their goals. Slowly increasing the amount and intensity of physical activity while cutting back on the amount you eat will result in weight loss.

Simple? Well actually it is that simple. What is going to get in the way is a factor that is not accounted for on a spreadsheet. You.

"My husband gave me an emerald ring after Ryan's birth. I use it as a constant reminder of him in my life and, when I feel the urge to binge on cherry cheesecake, I notice my ring and remind myself that I need to find some inner strength. Sure everyone else is eating it, but they didn't have a baby five months ago. It's like tying a knot in your tie or putting a string on your finger – it's just a lot more expensive."

"Snacking had become a habit I needed to break. Every time I felt like a snack, I drank a small bottle of mineral water and waited twenty minutes. By that time, I had either forgotten or was no longer interested."

Metabolic resistance to weight loss

There are a few medical conditions that inhibit weight loss. It's best to rule these out for peace of mind. These are factors to consider when you have tried everything to lose the kilos and your weight just isn't dropping.

THYROID MALFUNCTION

The thyroid gland's primary role is to regulate the speed of your metabolism. An irregular thyroid can flare up after childbirth, so don't rule this out if you have never had it before. It can be either over- or underactive. Symptoms of an overactive thyroid (hyperthyroid) include dramatic loss of weight, particularly while breastfeeding.

An underactive thyroid (hypothyroid) will do the reverse. Symptoms will be an inability to lose weight, sensitivity to cold, hair loss, fatigue, depression, dry skin, constipation, breaking nails, bad skin and high cholesterol. Your doctor will give you a blood test to measure your body's production of thyroid hormone and diagnose you accordingly. Underactive thyroid can be rectified by hormone supplements. Yoga is also extremely effective in regulating thyroid function.

USE OF PRESCRIPTION DRUGS OR HORMONES

A number of prescription drugs, particularly those that act as

"Without doubt, my biggest shock has been the change in my body. I am only twetny-eight, my daughter is one, and yet I feel like I aged years from the birth. I have grey hair coming through; I feel unfit, untoned and unattractive. I feel getting back my body and vitality is like climbing Mount Everest. I don't even know where to start."

antidepressants, can seriously stop dead your attempts to lose weight.

These include: oestrogen and birth control pills, diuretics, beta-blockers and antidepressant drugs, particularly the popular SSRIs (selective seratonin reuptake inhibitors) such as Prozac, Paxil (sold as Aropax in South Africa), Zoloft, Cipramil and Luvox. Generics include Lily Fluoxetine, Nuzac, Lorien and Prohexal.

INSULIN RESISTANCE

At any given time there is around a teaspoon of sugar in your blood. This level is maintained by insulin. What is not needed is stored as fat. When you drink a Coke your body is suddenly flooded with sugar. Now it is up to your pancreas to produce insulin to quickly reduce the blood sugar to appropriate levels. This means you will have a lot of insulin running around trying to get rid of the sugar. It can happen that your body becomes desensitised to insulin and it can no longer efficiently move sugar into your cells. This is more common in people who are significantly overweight.

CANDIDA

Candida albicans is the name of one of the hundreds of organisms that live in our digestive tracts. It is also very opportunistic

" I took fat burners for six weeks after I stopped breastfeeding. Ryan was ten months and I wanted to do something to shift the fat. I asked around and found one without ephedrine and started with one tablet before each meal. I raised that to two and didn't increase it further. It helped me control my appetite and shrink my stomach fast. I dropped at least four kilograms in six weeks, and then went on to retain control over my eating after that. "

"Everyone told me my body would never be the same again. When Tristan was four, I did the Body-for-Life Challenge. Within three months, my body was in better shape than when I was sixteen. I am more muscular, fitter and healthier as a mom than I have ever been in my life."

and can grow out of control. Pregnant women are extremely susceptible to candida. Apart from displaying as a red and itchy vaginal rash, candida can be present in the blood and intestines, where it interferes with the digestion and absorption of nutrients and can hamper attempts at weight loss. There are allopathic drugs, topical creams or pessaries on the market that will relieve the itch and knock your yeast levels back into shape for a while. But longer-term management is required to balance your body's levels of yeast. A combination of probiotics (acidophilus) that will put back the good bacteria and a spartan, sugar-free, yeast-free diet is the only real long-term solution. There is little medical evidence to prove this, but most women, nutritionists and homeopaths will say this is the best way to keep candida under wraps. You can find a lot of information online about candida diets or consult a homeopath or doctor for holistic treatment.

START THE MELTDOWN

1. Rule out a medical condition that could be stopping weight loss.
2. Cut portion size.
3. Start exercising.

Ten things every girl should know to lose weight

1. Every diet works, for a while. A high protein diet works, a low fat diet works, a high fruit diet works. Any diet in which you reduce your calorie intake is effective. You will lose weight in the short-term if you stick to ANYTHING. The question is not only what is right for you, but also what you can sustain with your lifestyle. Unfortunately few of these diets are sustainable over the long-term and, as older eating habits return, the weight will creep back on.

2. Eat less, weigh less. Now we can talk around this for hours, but unfortunately it really is true. As a rule, the law of physics does not lie. The vast majority of overweight people eat too much, but if you expend more energy than you consume, you will lose weight.

3. Drastic diets don't work. Dieting slows down your metabolism. The less you eat the more effective your body will get at using less energy. It will store the little you do eat and hold on to it for dear life. This is not good. The primary sins are skipping meals, fasting and dramatic changes in diet. Don't go on a diet; change your lifestyle.

4. Dieting is about being sensible. People think it cannot be that easy. There must be a trick to losing weight, a secret thin

"The biggest mistake I made during my pregnancy was to stop all exercise. From training five times a week, I literally stopped dead for nine full months. I interpreted my midwife's urges on me to take it easy as 'sit on your bum'. I continued with yoga, but absolutely nothing else. By the time I was about to give birth, I had gone from fit and strong to fat, self-loathing and out of touch with my body."

people know and we don't. Wrong. Losing weight is innately sensible, we are just bombarded with so many theories to try and make it easier that we are confused. We all know we will lose weight if we eat less.

6. There is no such thing as a quick fix. They are no quick fixes in the long run. Dieting is ninety-five per cent unsuccessful within five years. As a rule of thumb, it's reasonable to lose ten per cent of your body weight in a year. That means if you are tipping the scales at seventy kilograms, a good loss will be seven kilograms a year. That is just over half a kilo a month. Sound slow? Sounds good if it stays off.

7. Your genes rule. The strongest factor determining your body type will be your parents. Sorry.

8. It is very easy to be fat. Food is everywhere in this culture of instant gratification. We do not know what true hunger is.

We don't know what is in what we eat. There is little natural left in our world. The food we buy comes off supermarket shelves and has been mass produced, intensively farmed or manufactured on a production line with bottom lines and investors' interests at heart, not our health. We are being plied with hidden fats, sugars and salt in every morsel we buy. There is so much added fat in the food we eat, it's little wonder we have to fight to hold a healthy weight.

9. Carbs are not really the enemy. Sure most low-carb diets are effective for weight loss. If you cut out carbs you are cutting sugar, chocolates, biscuits, toasted sarmies, pizza, pastries, toast with butter. If you don't lose weight, there is a problem.

10. Don't get into the habit of thinking one food group is to blame for your weight. More often, overeating is the cause. But it sure sounds more hip to pass the pizza over saying: "I don't eat wheat," rather than: "I'm dieting."

" I ran a half-marathon twelve weeks after my birth. It was possibly crazy, but I felt fit and ready. I was back in the gym after six weeks and running five kilometres a day, but then I did a 45-minute spinning class the day of my birth. "

Get moving, Hilda Hips

If you want to lose weight, exercise is non-negotiable.

- Any type of exercise will speed things up. It can only be better than sitting on the couch or scoffing cake.
- Pace yourself. Start slowly and increase your intensity and duration over time. If you exercise too hard, too soon after delivery, your vaginal flow (lochia) may increase or turn red – a signal to slow down.
- Set an intention. For maximum results, work towards something. It may be health, better quality of life, a half-marathon or a spinnathon.
- Rope in your friends. Choose friends who will push you, not suggest you skip the session and have a skinny latte instead.
- Include weight-bearing exercises in your workout. Aim to boost your resting metabolic rate by increasing your lean body mass while burning calories. The ratio of muscle to body mass is what is going to make your metabolism rise.

TIP

If you're breastfeeding, exercise when your breasts aren't full of milk. For comfort and extra support, wear a sports bra over a nursing bra.

Diet Q & As

CAN HOT AND SPICY FOODS SPEED UP MY METABOLISM?

No. The thinking goes something along the lines of – chillies will kick-start your metabolism and fat burning. It may work if you eat a kilogram of bird's-eye chilli seeds every day, which is impossible of course. Remember: what goes in, must come out! Just think logically for one second before you hit those green Thai curries.

WILL EATING GRAPEFRUIT OR VINEGAR BURN CALORIES?

No food can burn up calories or melt away body fat. There is nothing magical about grapefruit or vinegar.

WHAT ABOUT ALCOHOL?

The jury is out on this. Our friend Atkins says that alcohol contains no impact carbs, while most so-called sensible diets will outlaw drinking. Diet expert Nicole Saks says that our bodies have no capacity to store alcohol. In fact, your body sees it as a poison and will try and get rid of it as soon as possible by flushing it out of the system, by using every scrap of water you are storing.

Alcohol makes food fattening. It goes hand in hand with a rich meal, a fistful of chips, a bag of peanuts and a late night stop at McDonald's. What's worse is that it distracts your digestive system on a physiological level. While it is desperately trying to siphon the poison out of your system, it's not paying much attention to digesting all the food and fatty snacks you have just packed in.

> " I have always been underweight and my post-pregnancy body has suddenly got a bum. I love it. "

WILL FAT BURNERS OR BINDERS HELP?

It looks seductive: the 'after' shot of a still heavy lass holding up a supermarket-bought outsize sundress who testifies to having lost sixty-eight kilograms in six months. "... And I didn't change my diet one bit," she says, snapping the now loose elastic waistband.

The claim is they grab carbs or fat in the food you eat and bind the evil substances to their chemicals, allowing them to pass through your system undigested. Fat binders are made up of chitin, a polymer found in crustaceans, which is easily digested by the body. This may work in a test tube. It does not in a body.

ARE APPETITE SUPPRESSANTS AND METABOLISM BOOSTERS GOING TO HELP?

Now, these do work over a short-term. They work to suppress your appetite, which can be effective in shrinking your stomach and getting you down to a smaller portion size. But they are not sustainable and are actually dangerous for you, with high doses of caffeine and a cocktail of stimulants that may have you snapping everyone's heads off. Stay clear of any with ephedrine (also known as ephedra and Ma Huang), as it's a central nervous system stimulant with reportedly damaging side effects. Ephedrine is banned in South Africa; however, the ban has not been effectively enforced and products containing ephedrine are often still available on shelves.

"My waist is a whole ten centimetres wider five years after giving birth for the third time."

my story: Kim

I have always been tiny, but in the year after I had Liam I became a walking skeleton. In the first week after my baby, I was back in my jeans. I thought this was fantastic and my friends were jealous as hell. But the weight loss didn't stop there. My baby refused a bottle and was unbelievably attached to my breast. As he fed, I got thinner and thinner. I had breastfed for seven months when I was walking down the beach with my best friend and her baby and I realised I looked like a walking corpse. When we got home after the holiday, I forced Liam to wean. I started to feel better, but my weight continued to fall. I decided I'd better go and see a doctor because everyone was asking me if I was sick. He told me that my body had stopped absorbing nutrients and that it is going to take time to come right.

He told me that my weight should be about fifty-one kilograms. I have always been a small person, weighing about forty-nine kilograms, but I was now weighing forty-five kilograms. An average person's body fat should be between twenty-three per cent and twenty-six per cent and in top athletes it's sixteen per cent. Mine was fourteen per cent. I was put on daily vitamin injections, tonics and a diet. As my body started to stabilise, I realised that I had felt like the walking dead for nine months. I still have not gained any weight, but I have stabilised. For a long time, the thought of another pregnancy made me feel physically sick, but I am starting to think I could do it again. But this time around, I would be carefully monitored so that does not happen again.

my story: Xoliswa

I have never been particularly thin, just normal really. I put on twelve kilograms with my second baby and eighteen months later, I had only lost four kilograms. That, added to the six kilograms I never lost from my first baby, meant I was no longer normal, I was fat.

I came home one day and my nanny's friend was visiting.

"Ooooh, look at you," she laughed. "You are so fat now." There it was, the cold, hard truth at last. I joined Weigh-Less the next day. The rebellious side of me was very agitated with doing things the 'normal' way. I hated weighing everything and having to think about what I was eating. I raged against the hard work to lose the weight. I fought my husband every step of the way. I hated having to plan meals and battled to fit it into my busy schedule. But I consistently dropped weight at around one kilo a week. Then people started commenting on how much weight I was losing. Because it was so slow, I never really noticed a dramatic change, but others did. The compliments and a self-congratulatory streak then kicked in and I wanted to lose faster. I abandoned Weigh-Less and went on to a protein diet. I did lose weight over the two weeks, but then boredom set in. I went on a backlash stuffing chips, bread and potatoes into my mouth at a rate of knots. I realised I was out of control and meekly went back to Weigh-Less. In six weeks, I had managed to regain almost all the weight I had lost. I was devastated and wanted to throw in the towel, but I knew I had to get this weight off, for my own sanity. I was warned it might take a while for my metabolism to stabilise after the crash diet. I stepped up my exercise and again started slowly losing. Over the next eight months, I dropped to my goal weight of sixty-four kilograms and have maintained that on the maintenance diet.

MOVE *your* MIND

When Ruby was eleven months, I told my husband I was ready to sell my convertible. I had bought it during a rash weekend two years before. While he was overseas for two short weeks, I changed our lives. I found a new house for us to rent and moved us in, I moved my office, I sold my old Golf and bought a convertible. I was so excited to drive it home, I only realised months later that I had paid R10 000 more than the price advertised in the paper. The salesman swears I misread the ad.

The second I fell pregnant, Llewelyn rushed off to price a station wagon. He came back with the deal almost in the bag.

"We will have to sell the convertible," he joyfully announced. This act threw me into a rage the likes of which he had never seen. He has certainly seen many of those subsequently. Station wagons were for horsey moms with three Jack Russells, cat hair on the upholstery and cooler bags with prepacked lunches. They were, in short, not for me.

CHAPTER 6

"I WILL NEVER SET FOOT IN A STATION WAGON. NEVER, NEVER, NEVER," I RAGED. He was baffled, still is. Surely this was a logical solution? He had all the reasons: it would be difficult getting the baby's car seat into a two-door car, the boot space was too small, and it wasn't safe.

It took me six months to work out that if I put the roof down and inched the driver's chair forward so my knees slipped under the cubby, I could load the pram into the backseat alongside Ruby. (We couldn't put it in the boot as we had splashed out on a pram that could comfortably house a 52-kilogram Rotweiller.)

This breakthrough meant I could take the pram out on excursions with me. It took twenty minutes to perform the insertion and equal time for the extraction, but it meant freedom.

Why did I hold on to my car like a pit bull? Did I love it? Not really. I think for a while I thought that this was the best damn car I would ever have and I was not going to let anybody tell me otherwise.

I also thought that I was not going to let this baby change my life in any way.

"It must fit in with my lifestyle, and this is part and parcel of who I am," I said. This child chose me for who I am, and a topless car, Hermes scarf and Gucci glasses were part of me. "Ruby would not want me to become an overly cautious, protective mom who cannot have fun or look glamorous." The reasoning went on.

"To this day, I have never felt gushy motherly love. What has developed is a strong, enduring love like I have never known. I will do whatever it takes to protect this child. Sometime, in the last five years, I finally accepted that I am his mother. I still consider it a job, one that I'll never resign from."

Within eight weeks of her birth, I was loading her into the car and doing all-nighters at an editing suite, finishing a documentary I had shot. Even hip moms keep to routine and I would bath her religiously at six every night and put her to sleep. Some nights this meant her bath was in the zinc kitchen sink at Gasworks post-production facility and a scrub down with the hand towel. Although I did not officially go back to my office, I worked just as hard as before from home.

I worked very hard at holding on to a life that had no meaning left for me.

I held on so long and so hard to my life, as I saw it, that the dawning reality that I was a mom only really kicked in when Ruby was six months.

And then, slowly, I started to accept that life was different now, accept it beyond coping with the sleepless nights, the hours alone in the nursery, the frustrations and the anger. I started to accept that I wanted it to be different, that I was different, that I no longer particularly wanted to down a bottle of tequila and throw up in the driveway or monopolise the dance floor with high-kicks and pole stroking, that I may have moved beyond weaving down the passage at eleven, two and five o'clock to feed her.

I wanted to do things differently than I had for the last twenty-nine years.

I started to realise that I was, gulp, a mom.

But I still won't reconsider the station wagon.

Lose yourself

Motherhood is one of the most powerful journeys a woman will go on and an underestimated transition in our culture. In the biological and physical sense, you become a mother almost instantly.

But there is a long road to becoming a mother in the spiritual sense. It is a hair-raising transition you may fight for months, or you may embrace it immediately. It may be a transition that you often question your commitment to, but make no mistake, little traveller: it's a one-way street and there is no going back. Here's what party girl Sadie Frost said: "My priorities have changed. I really enjoy making dinner for my kids and my husband – chopping ginger and marinating the tofu."

There is a belief that women will make a seamless transition from independent, social career girl to stay-at-home mom. But most moms will tell you there is nothing natural, seamless or serene about it. The centre of our lives is now a baby. Everything else will take second place for a while, including you.

Like the transition from human to vampire, you too must go through a process of death and of grieving to come to a new place.

Having a child is both a death and a birth. Both of them are yours to own.

The Jewish faith believes that a woman only starts the journey to reach her own potential when she has children. Indian women believe that there are special times in a woman's life when nature provides a narrow gap, an open window, for total rejuvenation of the physiology. These times follow your first period, menopause and the first six weeks after giving birth. At these times, your physiology is so delicate, so open and receptive, that you have the chance to recreate your health and heart.

The pregnancy and birth leave every cell depleted and it's up to you how you are going to fill them, to take you into the next cycle of your life.

"Being a mother has brought me the richest, deepest friendships of my life with other women. I absolutely know I can call up any number of people at any time of the night and they will be there for me. They know I need them and they need me."

Everyday grace

Baby showers, matric dances, twenty-firsts and weddings. In the long journeys of our lives, those are about the only benchmarks we actively mark and celebrate. And how do we do that? Most often with an open bar, store-purchased gifts and lots of money.

We have lost the simple art of ceremony, of celebrating transitions in life, of honouring our own journeys as women through our culture and of creating rites of passage. Never is it more needed than when you become a mom. A rite of passage is a simple act you plan, with intent to usher a new energy, stage, phase or idea into your life.

For the Hindu, life is a sacred journey and every step, from birth to death, is marked by a traditional ceremony called a samskara. These religious rites of passage are thought to direct life along the path of dharma. There are many types of samskaras from the rite prior to conception to the funeral ceremony. They are to mark clearly, within our minds, the occasion of an important life transition. Secondly, they are community outpourings of love, support and acknowledgement that allow the deeper meaning of life's transitions to sink into our souls.

Traditional Yemenite Jews celebrate the mother, thirty days after delivery, in a ceremony called *al-wafaa*.

" I knew I had to give up drinking. It was the eighth day in a row that I had woken up with a blinding hangover after a late-night party. I had been up, drunk and weaving down the passage three times since getting to bed in the early hours of the morning. I was fuzzy all day with a blinding headache. I spent the day snapping at my three-month-old baby and all I wanted to do was sleep. It was when I almost dropped her that I realised my drinking days were over. Nothing was worth that price. "

Guests gather at the house bringing plates laden with food and gifts for the mother and baby. Each guest sings and dances before the two, presenting wishes and blessings on them both.

Increasing numbers of young women are looking for ceremonies and traditions to create meaning in their own lives and to mark the passage of their growth. They are creating their own ceremonies and starting, for their own families, a legacy of celebration of life that goes beyond Cardies prepackaged messages. Many women are borrowing ceremonies and traditions from religions, others from age-old practices long forgotten, and others still are creating their own.

Space clearing

The power of ritual in creating a transition in your life is profound. Your home is your expression of self and the energy it holds has an effect on your wellbeing. It was the space you occupied as a newlywed, then as a pregnant woman and you need to shift the energy, to fill it with new light and energy for your role as a mom.

"When Lucy was six months, I did a personal growth workshop that challenged all my fears. I was hanging off a bungee cord, with my head dipping into the river, when I finally realised; I'm alive."

Many women instinctively find themselves moving home over a pregnancy or during the first year. It's a way of clearing your space, creating a new space and acknowledging that things are different and you need different surroundings. Space clearing is a ceremony you can perform yourself to say goodbye to the old and welcome in the new you.

You can do the whole house, but focus first on spaces that are uniquely you. Start with your bedroom. It's your space and sanctuary and a clearing can bring new life into your relationship.

- First create a blessing altar in the room, with a lit candle, beautiful fresh flowers, objects of meaning and some incense.
- Thoroughly clean the space before you start, washing down walls, wiping down all surfaces, airing cupboards and opening all the windows. Get rid of all clutter; throw away dead or dying plants and any broken objects or old magazines. Do it yourself.
- Cleanse yourself with a good bath.
- Traditional space clearings are done walking around the room in a clockwise motion and moving through all spaces with objects that create sound (bells, chimes, singing, chanting, prayer, blessings or intentions said for the room and your family or a special CD); that give new smells (smudge sticks, incense, water scented with aromatherapy oils that you can sprinkle); or that move air and energy (sweeping feathers or bits of silk cloth, blowing, moving your hands through the air).

If ringing bells or waving incense is not your style, then a simple act like repainting a room, washing all the curtains and furnishings and giving it a thorough spring-clean is a way to bring new energy and life into your home. If you act with intent, you can bring blessings and love into a space that seemed stagnant and dull. You can also choose a particular method like feng shui, or hire an expert or sangoma if you don't want to do it yourself.

Soul food

Throughout nearly all of human history – across cultures, continents and creeds – food has been considered sacred. The end of food means an end to life. Farmers prayed for rain, for protection

"After years of Ecstasy, recreational coke, clubs and cigarettes, I became a vegan. My journey to motherhood was so profound that I found myself along the way and lost all the shit I had thought was enlightening."

> *"I left my daughter when she was eight months old and travelled to Botswana, to undergo a sangoma training. I was back and forth over the course of six months. Everyone looked at me like I was a child abuser, but I had a drive to do this that changed the course of my life."*

from pestilence and for good harvests. Men fought and died for land. Land meant food. People honoured deities and gods with offerings of fresh fruit and gave blessings before consuming meals. Thanks was given to ancestors watching over the earth and ensuring enough food for all.

There is little sacred about the way we feed our bodies or our families today. Not only do we buy, but we also eat without intention and without thanks. Little wonder the world is getting fat, depressed and out of touch with the natural cycle.

Rethinking the role of something as simple as food and practising conscious eating can start to bring conscious thought into your everyday life.

Diet has an intimate connection with the mind because the mind is formed from the subtlest portion of the essence of food. Your inner nature becomes purified by the purity of food.

Here are a few guiding factors that can help you choose a *sattvic* and holistic, balanced diet.

- Take simple and natural food.
- The more you think about food, the more you will become body-health conscious.
- Always choose clean, uncontaminated, fresh and non-processed food.
- Food should be free from preservatives as they generate a lot of toxins in our bodies and our bodies have to work very hard to get rid of them.

" I became so serious, I hated myself. My first answer to any question was no. For my birthday, my husband organised a skydiving course for me. I resisted until the second I jumped and then my heart just burst with all the fun I hadn't let myself have as a mom. "

- Always try and choose organic foods or grow your own. This way, you will be saved from eating foods that are grown using chemical fertilisers and powerful pesticides that cause diseases.
- Sugar is recommended in its natural form only, via fruits, vegetables and grains.
- Finally, an essentially vegetarian diet is considered ideal because it not only makes you healthy but also gives you emotional and mental strength and uplifts you spiritually. Meat is not forbidden but the "fear energy" still present in the meat from mass slaughter is not beneficial.

Touch yourself

Somehow, we have come to think of massage as something a technician in a white tunic does to us as we lie on a bed, surrounded by incense and oils. Lovely, but a luxury. In fact, self-massage is practiced every day without your even noticing it – you stroke your forehead if you have a headache, rub your neck when you are tired or knead your leg when you get a cramp.

Massage is a therapy that combines touch, movement and energy. Of all the healing arts, it is one of the oldest and simplest; evidence of its use can be traced back to 3000 BC and in texts throughout the centuries, records are kept of massage being used as a healing and recovery process on the body, mind and soul.

FACT BOX

IN THE INDIAN TRADITION, THERE ARE THREE CLASSES OF FOOD:

Sattvic foods: These foods help to maintain health, increase strength, vigour and vitality and create balance. They include fresh fruit and vegetables, salads, lentils, yoghurt, milk, butter, wheat, rye, barley, nuts, rice and honey.

Rajasic foods: These foods are of medium quality and often processed. They generate passion and boisterous tendencies. They include sugar, meat, fish, eggs, coffee, cocoa, chillies, prepared mustard, cheese, spices, highly seasoned foods and foods that are excessively hot. Bitter, sour, salty and pungent foods, white sugar, radishes and deep fried food are all *rajasic* foods.

Tamasic foods: These are low-quality foods and make one inert and lazy. Beef, pork, all intoxicants, all drugs, alcohol, tinned foods, fizzy drinks, snacky foods, all stimulants, garlic and onions, stale, rotten and unclean foods, half-cooked and twice-cooked foods and mushrooms are all *tamasic* foods.

" *Four years after the birth of my son, I still looked and felt pregnant. When a friend invited me to join her on a three-month hike in Peru, I jumped at the chance. I knew the trip, at some level, would save my life. I was terrified to leave my son, but I was fighting for myself.* "

Many Indian women have a daily practice of *abhyanga* or self massage, said to promote the elimination of toxins and improve circulation and youthful skin. In fact, they view a daily massage as a critical part of postpartum recovery, to assist the body increase its circulation and get rid of toxins and fluids. The ideal oil to use is sesame, as it is a cleansing oil.

You should ideally spend ten to twenty minutes on the massage, with at least five minutes on your head. But you can get it done in five minutes if pressed.

- Warm a bottle of sesame oil and stand in a warm room.
- Start with your scalp and briskly massage in a motion like you are washing your hair.
- Gently move down and massage your face, smoothing away wrinkles with calming strokes.
- Pay attention to your ears, massaging the folds.
- Do the front and back of your neck with upward strokes.
- Now apply remaining oil to the rest of your body so it has maximum time in contact with your skin.
- Massage your arms using long up-down strokes over your bones and circular motions over your joints.
- Massage your chest, breasts and abdomen with sweeping, circular strokes. Over the abdomen use clockwise strokes, following your bowel pattern.
- Reach back and work your back and buttocks.
- Move down to do the legs with particular attention to your ankles and feet.

After the massage, you should leave the oil on for twenty minutes, ideally while you lie down somewhere warm and rest. Then have a hot bath or shower and rinse.

Move it sister

The basis of healing arts such as yoga and Tai Chi (qi gong) is movement. There is a gap in belief between Eastern and Western thinking on healing. Eastern practitioners believe that movement heals and that we need to move to bring qi – air, breath, chi or vital energy to address the problem. Western doctors believe stillness cures and will confine patients to bed, bind sore limbs or recommend rest.

Thousands of years ago we innately realised that movement was both part of life and a path to healing. Chinese, Africans, Aborigines and Indians all created their own methods to release stiffness and negative energy, increase circulation and to combat pain and headaches. Over the years, many of these dances become more systematised and structured, informed by nature and practice. Eastern thought also holds that as movement (yang energy) heals, so too does stillness (yin), which is why healing forms of movement embrace time for both stillness and motion.

Honour your body by taking up some weekly form of healing art.

"I walked out of my house when Ruth was two years old and did not stop walking. I took nothing, not my purse or a jersey. I walked till night and then slept under a bridge. I walked and hid for four days with tears streaming down my face until I had cried myself dry. Then I was ready to go home."

Dancing queen

Dance is a powerful way to get in touch with your body, your sensuality and your natural rhythm. It can be sexy, powerful or poignant, but it shifts you out of your rational mind and into a space of feeling and soul. You can sign on at the nearest Arthur Murray and learn the tango or you can look at some of the newer dance forms that combine the art of heart and healing with the power of movement.

Nia is a dance form from Hawaii that combines the healing, the artistic, the powerful and the creative. It is a movement technique designed for everybody to move in the way they are meant to move, organically and from their authentic centre.

Biodanza is a South American organic dance form that hails from Chile. It is a sensuous, sexy and physical way of getting back your body-mind connection.

Meditation

Meditation has been used for thousands of years to work towards spiritual enlightenment. The Americans got hold of it quite some time ago and have turned it into a national pastime. Their method of choice is transcendental meditation, a mantra-based form that induces deep calm and promotes healing.

Everyone has experienced a state of deep calm, open awareness or contentment at some point. Worries disappear, and your mind is clear and focused. This is meditation. With meditation, you can learn to deliberately return to that clear and open state. You can also learn to relax quickly and effectively, improve concentration and cultivate a deep sense of well-being and happiness. There are many forms of meditation from guided meditation, Buddhist open-eyed meditation to chanting and rocking.

Yeah, right, you are thinking, please tell me when I will find the time? Well, you need to be flexible during the first few months and squeeze in a few moments whenever you can. Some mothers use breastfeeding as a gap to close their eyes and focus on their own breath and body. Others just take ten minutes out when the baby takes a nap, or use a long bath as a place to unwind.

" I stopped eating one day and didn't start again for three weeks. I have never done anything like that before; in fact, I did not know it was medically possible. But I felt alive again, after four years of going through the motions and looking after a small boy. Now I fast one day a week. "

Sweat it

We are sanitised and deodorised and do not sweat enough. A sweat lodge ceremony, older than recorded history, is practiced in some form by every culture in the world. From ancient Roman baths and Mayan sweat-room ruins to Finnish saunas and Turkish baths, the evidence of the healing power of heat is everywhere. The medicine of sweat is most widely practised by Native American tribes who traditionally perform sweat-lodge "rebirths". The physically challenging act is as much for purification, cleansing and healing of the mind, emotions and spirit as it is for the body. The journey into a sweat lodge can be a life-changing event – a return to the womb and a rebirth of self.

The journey of a guided sweat lodge is profound for the body, mind and spirit and is not recommended until postpartum bleeding stops. Most tribal lodges will not allow women to sweat during their "moon". Physical effects of sweating can be: removing excess water caused by retention of salt, relieving aching muscles and cleansing the body. Bacteria and viruses cannot survive at temperatures much higher than 37°C. The rise in temperature also stimulates the endocrine glands and facilitates the release of negative ions into the air inducing relaxation and alertness.

Check the resources section for alternative health directories. Otherwise get yourself into a sauna regularly.

" I went hunting. I was somehow drawn to the primal, animalistic act in it. I have never hunted before but I shot a springbok, covered myself with its blood and ate its heart. My husband was half delighted, half horrified. I felt, being a mommy, I had lost touch with my animal side and it came out, in a way I never dreamed. "

SALT

How many kinds of tears are there? Is there a limit to them? Is there a point at which you will be all cried out? What is grief without tears? Does it look and feel different? Is it any less cleansing, less healing?

For the first nine months of your life, you were suspended in a sack of salty water and in the weeks after you give birth, you will return to that place. Water will surround you in the form of endless tears. They will pour down your face, washing your old life away, their salt bringing the sacred out of your heart and allowing it to flow back into the world.

Salt is a rock that sits, purified and disguised on your table. But in its white powder hides the secret to life. It is a substance that once drove empires to war and in some places and times, was valued more highly than a man's life. Its mythical power inspired philosophers and magicians, while its chemistry and rarity captivated science. Homer called salt a "divine substance". Plato described it as "especially dear to the gods". The Celtic word for salt is "holy" or "sacred". From the beginning of recorded history, salt was exalted and synonymous with virtue, purity and life. It was so precious that spilling it was considered a bad omen.

It is essential to all life; it regulates fluid balance and is necessary for movement, nerve impulses, digestion and healing of wounds.

All vertebrates have the same amount of salt in their blood (nine grams per litre), which makes it four times saltier than seawater. Salt plays a vital part in every cell of the human body and the ideal amount of salt for human babies is found in human breast milk. Salt is in your blood, amniotic fluid, sweat and tears. Its power in ritual and cleansing goes across culture and belief.

my story: Shelva

I truly became a mother when my baby was seven months old. My moment did not come when he was born, or over the long nights as I did my best to care for him. I went through all the motions and did all the things. I knew he was my baby. I knew I must care for him and protect him and I just kept going. I loved him because I had to. I was a mother technically and physically but not emotionally and spiritually.

The moment I truly became a mother was when my husband turned to me and asked one morning: "Do I still come first?" I knew as he asked that this question would change my life. My heart was pounding; my body, heart and soul knew the answer I had resisted for a long time. The answer was, no.

"No."

Zach comes first. I knew then that this child was truly my first priority, my deepest love, my bravest journey and my clearest reason for living. I had resisted it for a long time. I had taken my time and accepted it on my own terms. It did not mean that my husband came lower on my list or that he got less love. Nor does it mean I rate myself, or my needs, any lower on my scale. There is no scale, just an endless well of love of which there is no bottom. Enough love for me, for my husband and for each of our children.

I know that perhaps it won't always be like this, that years down the line someone else will come first, maybe I will again. But I do suspect that my child will, always.

I saw in that moment the hugeness of my own mother's heart, the incredible depth of her love through all the years. I knew that I would have that same binding to my son. I saw in that moment then, that we have a journey of a lifetime together and the knowledge gave me such excitement, I could hardly hold the energy in.

my story: Kate

I did a life-changing water fast and colonics. I had been dancing around the idea of fasting for years. Something about its discipline and the potential for a mind-shift appealed to me after years of spiritual exploration. My son was one and somehow I still felt like a dumpy frumpy mommy. I needed to do something radical to rediscover my body, my health and my vitality.

The day I went for my first consultation I was six kilograms over my pre-pregnancy weight. The fast was seven days of water and a variety of detoxifying potions. The first three days were truly hell. I was ravenous and then an incredible detox headache hit. But the experience of pregnancy and birth has given me an inner strength I had never had access to before. I just put my head down and did it. On day four, we started the colonics. I was totally relaxed about allowing a stranger to fiddle around my bottom and Bev, the

practitioner, made me feel comfortable about the experience.

After the first treatment, I walked out a changed person. I had witnessed a testimony to the years of poor eating that were released from my body. I was letting go of my old life. I felt like I was walking on air. The extraordinary amount of sludge that was evacuated from my body gave me renewed willpower. My hunger abated and I started to enjoy the incredible energy coursing through my body. I can't say I looked forward to the daily enemas, but I knew they were doing my body immeasurable good. On day seven, we did the last colonic. I had lost six kilograms of crap. I did not do the fast to lose weight, but the weight loss has been a bonus and has stayed off, six months later. The seven days showed me the power I have, to keep my word, to stick to an intention and to continually change myself if I want to.

my story: Rehana

I am a doctor and consider myself a modern, urban, Indian woman, but I chose to go to my parents' home and follow the rituals of their culture when I birthed my daughter. I saw nothing in Western medicine that brought the spiritual and the emotional into the birth of my child. I knew there was more and I felt that the rituals and traditions of my culture had more of an insight into what it meant to become a mother. I delivered in a hospital and was taken to their home in Lenasia to recover.

In my culture, this is not a time for men and the women of my family gathered to attend to me and my new baby. As I arrived back, I was anointed with henna. I lay resting while the elder women meticulously painted my nails. I had been painted before the birth like a bride. After the henna was painted on, I would rest for hours, not allowed to touch anything in case it smudged. This was our way of forcing me to rest and focus only on my baby.

For the first seven days, I was secluded with my baby and the women of my family looked after us. I felt blessed and special and I knew this was a far cry from the alienation my friends had described from their births. I felt revered and supported. On the seventh day, I was dressed, my hair and body was perfumed and my hands and feet hennaed before visitors streamed through our house for a great feast that went on for days. The house was decorated for blessings and in the courtyard, my aunt had drawn our religious deities, with flour, on the floor.

My husband joined me at my parents' house for the next two weeks, although the house was a place for women. We followed the tradition of abstaining from physical intimacy for forty days, although the three of us returned to our house after three weeks. My mother came with us to bring the old ways into our home. Many modern women are turning back to the traditional ways, where a ritual transition back into society is offered, rather than antidepressants or drugs.

SURGERY, SUCTION *and* SPAS

On and off went the third outfit. It's not like I was going anywhere, just trying to find something that looked like I was not on my way to check into an Overeaters Anonymous meeting. I stood, deliberating, in a pair of control-top pantyhose. They were not properly pulled up and were cutting off the circulation to my lower hip. The top half of my hip was hanging over the waistband in a lumpy roll. I turned to the bed and saw that my husband was looking at me with a quizzical expression. He had put his book down and had clearly been watching me for some time. I would have been comfortable with the expression if I were selecting a paint colour for the garden wall. But I was naked. Worse, I was wearing an undergarment that should only be revealed on pain of death.

"Are your boobs smaller?" he asked.
Deny.
Put on surprised smile.
"Are they?" I asked. "I hadn't noticed."
That did not do the trick.
"It's just like they are less … soft. Like they are the same, yet not the same."

CHAPTER 7

IT WAS THEN THAT HE OFFERED ME A BOOB JOB IF I THOUGHT IT WOULD MAKE ME FEEL BETTER. He had watched my tortuous coming to terms with my new body. I had always joked about having no objection to buying youth and pert breasts, but I was now being offered a very real choice. Somehow, I expected the choice to come when I was around fifty, not twenty-nine.

Who can blame a girl for considering going under the knife? These are the moments where that slush fund for a rainy day starts to show its benefits. Who says droopy boobs aren't a rainy day?

"It was a holiday for the two of us in the East – a three-week luxury trip, we had been saving for. I had all but forgotten the plans until Neville said he wanted to check dates with me to buy the tickets. A month later, I had a tummy tuck and breast augmentation and lift with the money instead," says Marcia. "Now, that's what I call a real holiday."

Perhaps we think that our fannies and pert boobs are with us for the long haul, with no service date. But this is not the case. While penoplasty has had its day in creating an awareness that there are surgical procedures out there for men and their not so dangly bits, there is little awareness that help is at hand for women who simply cannot, or do not want to, come to terms with a new body.

And frankly, it is cheaper to get that fat sucked out than to replace a wardrobe of couture. Or that's the party-girl line, and we are sticking to it.

If there is a trend that defines our postpartum physique, it is a distinct lack of tone. Everything is slack, from our previously taut tums to our vaginas.

There cannot be a new mother who has not caught sight of her tail and thought, "Whose rump is that?" And if your baby came out the sunroof, don't think you are any better off. Sure your vagina may not look like a giant, unstuffed cannelloni tube, but you are not going to escape all the "joys" of motherhood.

Let's refresh our memories:
- Flaccid belly
- No waist
- Thighs that fall in folds over your knees
- Slack fanny
- Droopy boobs

Childbirth is a trauma to your entire body. It is massive, invasive … and totally natural. But make no mistake, things can and frequently do, go wrong. More commonly, things don't go wrong, they just don't shrink back into place. Thank God we live in the twenty-first century where we can put them right.

Let's take a look at what you can do:

Vein removal

Spider veins: These are known by the white coats as telangiectasias or sunburst varicosities, and are those small, thin veins that lie close to the surface of your skin. They mostly clear within three months of a birth but can be permanent. Varicose veins are thicker, larger and darker, and they bulge.

If you think you might want vein removal surgery, you should wait until you've had all the children you want because, unfortunately, varicose veins tend to worsen with each pregnancy and with age.

" I was walking my daughter into playschool when the little boy walking behind me shrieked: 'Look mom, Lisa's mommy has veins outside her legs, like the Hulk. Gross."

TIP

A dead leg is not from lack of blood to your legs, it's too much blood. Chances are you have been sitting on your leg, stopping all that hard work to get the blood circulating. Help your body by elevating the limb.

THE OP

Sclerotherapy: In this rather simple but costly procedure, veins are injected with a solution that causes them to collapse and fade from view. The injection causes the walls of the vein to fuse over a period of a couple of weeks. The vein then shrivels up and is absorbed back into the body. Because surface veins carry relatively little blood, the body easily reroutes flow to deeper veins.

A typical sclerotherapy session can be done during your lunch hour and you will get between five and forty injections in a session – one for 2.5 cm of vein. Depending on the number and size of your enlarged veins, you may require several sessions. Afterwards, you'll most likely need to wear compression stockings from a few hours to a few weeks, to keep the shrunken veins from refilling.

Mini-stripping (ambulatory phletectomy): The doctor will make tiny incisions along the length of an enlarged vein. She then uses a hook to actually scoop out tiny sections of the vein.

Laser or needle: Laser surgery is also available and this works in a similar way. The heat generated by the laser causes the blood vessel to disintegrate. It's effective, but sclerotherapy is still more popular. Working in a similar way is a process similar

TIP

Always massage in an upward motion towards your heart. Firm rubbing downwards can damage a valve and is working against your body's own flow. Upward motions protect your valves and support your body to process blood and water in your extremities.

to electrolysis that involves zapping veins with high frequency waves that pass down a fine needle and into your vein.

THE CATCH?

It's not cheap, costing a couple of thousand rands a leg. But it can be done with a local anaesthetic, on an outpatient basis. The procedure carries the usual risks of undergoing surgery, including a small possibility of scarring and infection.

These fixes aren't permanent. If you got varicose veins once, you may get them again. The surgery has its own dangers, including infection and scarring at the injection sites, but they are relatively rare. Some women have reactions to the solution. Expect some temporary bruising. A lot of women find they remain with pigmentation marks in the area for up to two years.

THE COST

The cost of the procedure varies greatly depending on how much time is spent in theatre and whether or not it's done on an outpatient basis. Grab the credit card and get a thorough breakdown from your doc.

Slimming clinics

The costs of salon work are a fraction of what you would spend on surgery, but this is still not an alluring option if you are on a tight budget.

Your post-birth bulk can be targeted on two fronts.
1. Break down fat and cellulite with a G5 slimming machine. This hand-held device vibrates over your fat like a jackhammer. You know what a jackhammer does to tar? Well, this will purport-

" After each of my three boys, I went for muscle toning sessions for about six weeks. I am naturally slim and the salon just helped me cut down on the time it took my stomach to reduce and tone. "

edly do the same to your fat. It then leaves it up to your lymph system to flush out the broken-down fat. It will most certainly get the circulation going in those areas; not a bad thing.

2. Tone your slack stomach muscles with passive exercise toning pads. These go under various brand names but essentially send electrical impulses to your muscles, causing them to contract and spasm. Feels mildly strange but nothing too alarming. Salons claim it's as effective as three hours in the gym.

THE CATCH?

This will only work if you are prepared to work with the programme. You cannot strap yourself to a vibrating machine while slurping a milkshake. Stick to a calorie-controlled diet and an exercise programme and you will see results. Otherwise, don't waste your money.

THE COST

A G5 session will set you back R70 for thirty minutes and you are in for a minimum of ten sessions. Toning machines go for around R90 for forty-five minutes. For best results, you need to do both, three sessions a week. Anything less than ten sessions on either will have little effect, so you are looking at a minimum of R1 600, although packages sell at reduced rates.

Breast lifting (mastopexy)

This is a lift. It will give you higher, not larger, breasts. If you want both, you need to combine a breast lift with implants. If, on the other hand, you have large breasts and would like them lifted and reduced, this is possible; skin or tissue can be removed at the same time as the lift. Wait until you have had all your children before you opt for breast surgery as round two may set you back to square one.

A mastopexy can be performed under local or general anaesthetic. It can be performed as an outpatient procedure and you will be home within a few hours of surgery. It's a lot less painful than implants even though the cuts are larger.

THE OP

The surgeon will make an anchor-shaped incision, going along the underside of your breast and up to your nipple. The skin will then be gathered, excess skin cut off, and the site will be stitched. Your nipple and aureole will be reattached higher on your breast.

THE CATCH?

Surgery carries risk. Your breasts will be bruised and swollen, but the pain is not severe. Some women may have numbness in the aureole or a change in sensitivity in the entire area, particularly the nipple. Scarring will depend on the surgeon and your own scarring capacity, but scars can remain red, raised and unsightly. You could also be left with unevenly positioned nipples.

You should also keep in mind that a breast lift doesn't keep you firm forever. Skin does age and stretch.

THE COST

It will cost around R19 000 for the surgeon, anaesthetist, one-night stay in a clinic and all peripheral costs. If you add on an enlargement or reduction, you are going to pay more.

TIP

For any work on your breasts, it is vital that you find a surgeon who comes recommended. Plastic surgery is part science and part art and not all surgeons are created equal, Dr Jekyll. See the box, Choosing a surgeon, on pg 161.

Breast enlargement (augmentation)

Most women will have smaller breasts after pregnancy, whether they breastfeed or not. During pregnancy, the milk glands in your breasts swell and actually replace the fatty tissue that gave your breasts a full, soft look. When you stop breastfeeding, the glands shrink, leaving you with less bulk than before. This will cause the breasts to look less full or sag. A breast enlargement is not a lift.

If you want your breasts higher on your chest, you will need to combine an enlargement with a lift. Although, bear in mind, the implants will give them a firmer shape in any case.

THE OP

This is done under either local or general anaesthetic and you can check out the same day, though an overnight stay is recommended. A small incision is made in each breast and a cavity created inside your breast. The small incisions are virtually undetectable and are usually made under each breast around the nipples or in the armpits. Implants may be inserted just under the gland of the breast or beneath the muscle tissue. Stitches are removed after approximately a week.

All breast implants now in use consist of a silicone shell, which is either factory-filled with silicone gel or is filled during

"I decided to have a lift when Josh was two. I had regained my figure but my breasts had gone from a full B cup to barely an A. And they were not small pert breasts. They were small and sagging. The operation was painful. When the swelling finally went down I had pert breasts. But then I started to feel they were too pert. My nipples are too high on my chest. If I wear a string vest top, my nipples peak over the top of the shirt. To rectify it will take another, more complicated, operation that I am just not up for."

surgery with saline. Other fill materials are being investigated experimentally. Despite ongoing reports in the media, the Association of Plastic and Reconstructive Surgeons maintains there has never been a systemic illness definitively attributed to silicone implants. Mothers with implants can breastfeed with no risk to the baby.

The implant is placed either behind the major pectoral muscle that runs down your chest, or in front of it. The problem with placing it in front of the muscle is that your body's healing mechanisms may be too powerful and scar tissue can surround the implant, making the breast appear as if it has a hard lump.

" I was most surprised by how painful the recovery was. My doctors said it would be sore, they didn't tell me quite how sore. "

THE CATCH?

- You need a week off work to allow for adequate recovery.
- The pain – breathtaking. It far outstrips the pain of a breast lift.
- A small percentage of women develop an infection around an implant. This may occur at any time but is most often seen within a week after surgery. If antibiotics are not effective, the implant may need to be removed for several months until the infection clears. A new implant can then be inserted.
- Concerns regarding the long-term safety of silicone remain. The US Food and Drug Administration banned silicone gel implants over a decade ago. It reinforced the ban in 2003 despite a vote from its advisory panel to lift it because of a lack of evidence.

THE COST

It will cost you between R19 000 and R25 000 for the surgeon, clinic, anaesthetist and materials.

Tummy tuck/stomach tightening (abdominoplasty or lipectomy)

"My entire torso has got a shape again."

A tummy tuck is the big sister of liposuction and entails actually removing a bulk of sagging skin and fat. If you are at your ideal weight, have done more sit-ups than Britney Spears and your stomach area is still a loose, flabby mass of skin, stretchmarks and scarring, you can start looking at abdominoplasty.

These operations are usually very successful.

THE OP

The surgeon will start with a cut that goes from hip to hip and a separate cut to free your navel from the skin.

Next, your skin is lifted off the abdomen, starting just above the groin and going up to near the rib cage, to expose the abdominal muscles. These will be pulled closer together and stitched into position. Then skin is then pulled down and inwards, the excess skin is cut off and the remaining skin sewn back into place. A new super-neat bellybutton will be created out of skin.

"It was a huge decision for me, but I could not face the kangaroo pouch with stretchmarks for another year. The scar is really significant, but it's lower than the stretchmarks and does not stick out of my jeans."

"I am twenty-nine years old, and I have a toned body, except for a revolting belly. I have had two pregnancies and it has taken its toll on my body. It changed the way I dress. I could not bear to look at my stomach. It disgusted me with its patchwork of stretchmarks and loose skin. No amount of exercise would have tightened the amount of extra skin I had. It was a tough decision to have the surgery, but it has changed my life. I can wear hipsters again and not feel a pang if my shirt rides up. I can face my husband without a shirt on."

If you have only a small amount of excess skin and it is limited to below your bellybutton, you may be a candidate for a mini-lipectomy (a less extensive procedure, often done under local anaesthetic), possibly combined with liposuction. Here, the operation will take place on a smaller scale and only below your navel. Full abdominoplasty will take up to five hours. A temporary tube may be inserted to drain excess fluid from the site.

THE CATCH?

Recovery is slow. This is a major op. You will stay in hospital for at least a day, or for up to a week, depending on the amount of skin and fat removed.

Anticipate booking four weeks off work. After ten days, you will be able to stand fully upright. Scarring will take up to six months to start to reduce.

The scar is large and permanent. It will run from hip to hip but usually under your bikini line. Severe scarring can occur and is usually due to genetic factors.

There will be a degree of numbness in the skin, but this should be temporary. Infection and clotting are risks, but they are rare and can be treated with drainage and antibiotics. Early movement will minimise the risk of clotting.

THE COST

This will set you back between R16 000 and R26 000 depending on the size of your stomach and the complexity of the operation. This includes hospital stay anesthetist, surgeon and a bellybutton reconstruction.

TIP

Make sure you are clear what the quoted generic price includes. Bellybutton reshaping is billed separately, as is work on muscles.

Spot fat reduction (liposuction)

Spot fat reduction is the most commonly requested cosmetic surgery procedure and is the last resort for moms battling to shake fat that won't move off their bellies, arms or thighs. There are immediate results, but the real results kick in after four months – many women describe the fat "melting off". If you don't follow an exercise and eating regime, you can regain the fat.

THE OP

This is usually done in hospital under either local or general anaesthetic, with a one-night stay-over. It can be done as an out-patient procedure. The safest route is the tumescent technique. A liquid mixture of saline, adrenaline and a local anaesthetic is injected into the area. Then two small incisions are made in your skin through which your surgeon will manipulate a tube attached to a vacuum machine. The fat is removed in tunnels – you will look like an Emmentaler cheese for a while. You will wear a compression garment for up to six weeks.

THE CATCH?

The first twenty-four hours after the operation are critical, as you have to take in enough water to compensate for the fat and fluid you have lost. It's over this critical recovery time that most headline grabbing "lipos-gone-wrong" happen. Any operation during which more than a kilogram of fat is removed warrants an overnight stay in hospital. Scarring is negligible. The younger you are, the better your skin will "shrink-wrap" after surgery. Stretchmarks indicate your skin has been overstretched or has poor elasticity; liposuction will not be as effective on you.

THE COST

A surgeon, anaesthetist and clinic, with a one-night stay-over will cost from R15 000 to R20 000. As an outpatient, you are looking at R8 000 to R10 000.

Labioplasty

This procedure is apparently gaining ground as Barbie dolls and Playboy centrefolds raise the bar for little labia.

As any crotch expert will tell you, there is actually no such thing as a "normal" labia minora (the inside lips); they vary as widely as noses, from small and pert to pronounced and proud. What started out as an operation to repair tears or trauma to the labia that can occur during delivery, has evolved into snipping your lips back for aesthetics' sake. This is Cosmetic with a capital C.

THE OP

Your plastic surgeon may perform this outpatient procedure under local or general anaesthetic. It will take about one-and-a-half to two hours.

The surgeon will perform a snip and trim on your labia minora, the flaps of skin that form the "lips" of your genitalia and cover the clitoris and vaginal opening.

Recovery takes only a few days.

THE CATCH?

Responsiveness during sex is not confined to the clitoris and comes from nerve sensors all over that area. This could mean you will sacrifice feel for form. Seems a pity.

SURGERY, SUCTION and SPAS

THE COST

This is a relatively small procedure, but it is done under a general anaesthetic, so you are looking are a minimum of R12 000 for the surgery and full crew.

Vaginal tightening

This is not a commonly requested or performed procedure even in Vegas. It involves cutting into the thick muscles that form your perineum, removing a wedge and then sewing them back together. Recovery is pegged at ten days.

THE CATCH?

It's surgery, so infection is always a risk. You are going to have to work those muscles to keep the tone. Not many people are going to comment on your results.

THE COST

Not many SA surgeons perform it, but costs are estimated at around R12 000 for an in-hospital procedure.

> **TIP**
>
> To avoid dizziness if you are standing for a while, sway back and forth. This will help your muscles pump the blood back up.

Skin pigmentation

Changes in skin pigmentation (chloasma) are common on the face during pregnancy. Some studies suggest that up to three in four women may develop chloasma, which is characterised by blotchy, brown patches.

If the discolouration is only on the outermost layer of your skin, you will start with a mild peel you do at home. Your dermatologist or beautician will give you a chemical exfoliating agent, such as Retin-A or glycolic acid, in increasing doses. Stronger acids such as alphahydroxy acid peels (AHA) are most often done in-salon.

Stronger peels will move beyond the epidermis and start to work on the second layer of skin, the dermis. These are for more significant sun damage and the chemical trichloroacetic acid (TCA) is painted on to your face. This is uncomfortable and requires seven to ten days of healing.

THE CATCH?

Put a foot back in the sun, and you will have wasted all that money. As we all know, exposure to the sun increases pigmentation, so unless you want a tan that looks as though it was done with a sponge by a bad interior decorator, stay in the shade. No *Sex and the City* fan will ever forget the disastrous results and flaking raw skin of Samantha's cosmetic catastrophe when she went for a face acid peel. "A refreshing chemical peel. It only takes fifteen minutes and can take ten to twenty years off your face," recommended her doctor.

THE COST

In-salon AHA peels start at R280 a session and you will need to go for a minimum of six to eight sessions.

Your medical aid does not cover any cosmetic surgery. On rare occasions, abdominoplasty may be partially covered if a medical-functional problem, such as a hernia or abdominal wall defect, is involved.

IS MY BOX TIGHT ENOUGH?

Your vagina is surrounded and supported by muscles. Like any body part, you can trim and tone it if you put some time in. It's a part of the body you are not used to working; this will change once you have had a baby. Healthy muscle tone will feel different to slack muscle tone. This will require the Finger Test. Now don't be coy ...

STRONG MUSCLES:

■ The canal is tight and the tissues offer your finger a degree of resistance from all directions.

When your finger is inserted to its full length, move around a bit, palpitating it against the walls.

– The walls should close in around the finger as it is inserted, moved about or withdrawn. This should happen as deep as you can move your finger not just in the first third of the canal.

– As you move your finger, the walls of the middle third of the normal vagina feel firm throughout.

– You will feel a strong contraction as you tense your muscles around your finger.

SLACK MUSCLES:

■ The entrance to the vagina may feel tight but this ends once you get two-thirds up.

Insert your finger:

– The canal will feel roomy; the walls will not close in on your finger or will offer little resistance to movements of your finger.

– Try and tense your muscles around your finger. If you barely feel it, you have some work to do.

CHOOSING A SURGEON

You don't find your gynae in the Yellow Pages. Equally, you would never consider a plastic surgeon without a recommendation from someone you trust. This is part science, part sculpture and results vary widely. Take your time to find the right surgeon. It is expensive and the results will last you a long time, so do it right.

- Ask your friends, ask your GP and ask the surgeon if you can call some recent patients.
- Don't select a surgeon purely because they are less expensive. You get what you pay for.
- Educate yourself. Get online and research all the variations of your op, know what can go wrong, interview a few surgeons on their techniques and grill them on why they do it that way.
- Check out their qualifications with the SA Plastic and Reconstructive Surgeons Association on 031 566 4100 or www.plasticsurgeons.co.za
- Check there are no malpractice suits against them. Call the Health Professions Council of SA on 012 338 9300.
- Ask all your questions and raise your fears.
- Make sure that you have been informed of all the costs.
- Ask who the anaesthetist will be and what drugs will be used.
- Be clear what aftercare is required and plan this.

www.plasticsurgery.org: This is a US-based website but has a good info section on all ops.

Vibrating Chinese balls work on your core vaginal muscles as they stimulate muscle contractions. Holding them in is more difficult than it seems. Don't wear them at work without knickers or you could be playing skittles in the corridor.

ARTERIES AND VEINS

Arteries carry fresh blood from the heart to every cell in your body, through a system of smaller and smaller vessels. These vessels then become tiny capillaries that pass almost every cell, delivering oxygen and nutrients. This network then collects the by-products of metabolism from these cells and starts to wind its way back to the heart. Capillaries join to form slightly larger vessels (venules, or tiny veins) and these in turn join up to form veins. All veins eventually join into two main veins that feed into the heart, one coming from the legs and pelvis (inferior vena cava) and the other from the abdomen (superior vena cava).

Your body has to work hardest to get the blood back up to your heart from your legs as it is working against gravity. Fortunately, the valves in your veins will only let blood flow upwards, towards your heart. Your leg muscles move the blood back up, not your heart pumping. A valve occurs every five to ten centimetres in the main superficial veins of the legs.

When veins become varicose, the valves often stop working properly; blood can flow the wrong way and cause a head of pressure that makes the veins bulge.

Varicose veins are not dangerous. They have nothing to do with thrombosis, heart attacks, strokes or any heart conditions. Having them treated is a cosmetic, not a health decision.

my story: Magritte

When I met my first husband, he told me one night that I had the most beautiful fanny he had ever seen. It was the first time in my life I had even thought about that part of my body as anything other than functional. We married a year later.

I had my first son in 1994 when I was twenty-four. The birth was a long and tough one and Rex was 3.9 kg. I ended up with a fourth degree episiotomy that cut me from vagina to anus. The stitches and cut hurt like hell for two years, and I battled infection after infection. I just put my head down and got on with my life and the challenges of being a mother. I put myself, my sexuality and ultimately, my marriage on the backburner. I was in pain and felt my fanny was ugly, scarred and damaged.

My relationship took a fatal blow in those years and we ended up getting divorced. I fell pregnant again the next year with Mark's baby. We had been dating for four months. Kevin was born at 4.1 kg and I had no problems. I knew in my heart it was because my vagina was so loose there was little stretch needed.

This time I worked hard to get it back into shape and went on a physiotherapy programme. I tried vaginal dumbbells, electromagnetic therapy, even vaginal beads, but the muscle was so numb from the scarring that I made no inroads. I felt like my fanny was a great roomy void.

Tampons would even slip lower as there was just no tone. I wanted to just ignore that part of my body, and I wanted my husband to ignore it as well. My husband said it made no difference to him, but it made the world of difference to me.

One day I read an article on an airline magazine about vaginal tightening. It was like a ray of light for me. I got online and started researching options. Eventually I contacted a surgeon in Canada who had performed a number of vaginal tightenings. He advised me to have all my children before I considered it.

Finally, last year I had my third son Seth.

When he was eight months, we flew to Canada for a "holiday". I checked in the next day and went under anaesthetic. I had my labia trimmed and my vagina tightened. I stayed the night and checked out the next day with minimal pain and we continued with our holiday. The area was bruised but bearable.

The surgery has made the world of difference to me and my sex life. The scar is barely visible and I feel as tight as an eighteen-year-old. Mark says the difference during sex is huge. Who knows if he is lying because he never really had a problem with our sex life before. The real difference is to my self-confidence. I am only thirty-four, and I have waited ten years to feel okay about my fanny again.

LIFE
in
THE PITS

You have taken three months off your job, glowed through the pregnancy, touched up your roots for the birth and squeezed in a Brazilian wax so it's all tidy for the event. You locked your glass corner office in front of your 200 staffers at the farewell breakfast they organised. They had to drag you out, if truth be told. "I'll be back," you snarled with your Austrian accent at its practised best. You know how to play for laughs.

So here you are at home with your new baby. Home alone. Everything looks the same. Same garden, same television, same fridge. But everything is different.

You are supposed to have beautiful skin, a smile on your face and a lovely baby attached to your breast. You are supposed to gaze beautifically at her and gently rock as you doze off to sleep together on a rug in the dappled afternoon shade. You are not supposed to be hysterical, frazzled, anxious, manic and desperately trying to hold it together. Everything is wrong, yet there is no reason. You had a perfect birth, you have a supportive and loving husband, you have a nanny waiting in the wings, a nursery full of everything that squeaks and glitters. So what is wrong? Why are you not coping?

CHAPTER 8

" I would see a homeless woman on the side of the road with a child and think: She is coping, she is a mother. I have it all, and I am pathetic. "

WELL, IT COULD BE THAT MOTHERHOOD IS A MASSIVE, EXHILARATING, wild roller-coaster ride of fear, love, frustration, anger, joy, sadness and every emotion in between. Or it could be that having a baby has triggered something you may never have experienced before: depression.

What is PND?

The deep depression women may fall into after childbirth has been documented as a condition for centuries, but until forty years ago it was seen as a unique or stand-alone condition only exhibited in postpartum women. In fact, it is not.

"Post-natal depression is actually a depression, like any other depression," says Dr Andrea Taub. "It just happens to be sparked by the birth of a baby, while at other times, triggers may be illness, loss, accident, drugs or an event.

Depression in general is seemingly unbearable at any point in your life, but the fact that this arrives when you are battling with a tiny baby, makes it such an incredibly loaded and terrifying experience. You are living in an emotional vortex in which all normality has been stripped away from your life, which is why the condition is so often undiagnosed."

"What is depression?" says Trish. "I was living in a parallel universe of nightmarish feeds, endless burping and sleepless nights. There was no normality at all on which I could rate my

" I was still drizzling at every second word on my fifth day in the hospital, when a psychologist arrived at my bedside. Subtle as a red-lipped tart, she virtually talked me into a depression. An hour after she left, I checked myself out. Sure I was emotional, but I was not depressed. "

behaviour and myself. I thought things were just really tough. Depression didn't cross my mind for two years."

What does it feel like?

Doc Andy Taub describes two predominant types of depression.

ANHEDONIC DEPRESSION

This type of depression manifests as a sense of finding no pleasure in anything. You may just want to sleep, not want to get out of bed, feel tired, lethargic and passive. Ironically, this can often coincide with insomnia. Most often you will wake in the early hours of the morning when you will experience a deep feeling of despair. Eating patterns can manifest as either overeating or lack of hunger.

MANIA OR ANXIOUS DEPRESSION

With this type of depression, you feel so agitated and anxious you don't know what to do with yourself. Your body is on fire, your metabolism is racing away with you, but you don't want to eat. You feel like you could run the Comrades, but you can't get off the couch. You might drop weight at record pace, talk and interact at high speed, or feel as though you are immobilised and can't communicate at all. You may feel unmotivated to make plans as usual but may try to busy yourself to stop the feeling. This is the more common experience of PND.

" *I was in mid-sob, lying on the couch after five hours of crying, when my know-it-all older sister arrived. 'Oh good, day three,' she said. 'You'll be over this by tomorrow.' It was a relief to know I was normal but annoying that I was so predictable.* "

Mind games

"The word depression in post-natal depression is a misnomer that makes it difficult for women to diagnose themselves. It creates the assumption that you will feel down and depressed. However, the usual experience is that of extreme anxiety. This is not a passive depression; it is an activated, agitated depression. Your body is in a bizarre antithesis where you are in a state of frozen anxiety," says Doc Andy.

Anxiety is usually a vague imagining. It is not a concrete fear about losing your job or performing at a presentation but is more of a sinking feeling that something terrible is going to happen, that you are not okay. Most often, it manifests as dreadful, worst-case scenario imaginings – death, loss, illness or just vague future disasters. Some part of you knows these will not happen, and your rational mind tells you to stop. But your rational mind is not in control here.

Fiona (thirty-eight) is a highly successful TV producer with a four-year-old son. She says her incredible energy was the envy of all her friends.

"I was sleeping probably only three hours a day. Even when my baby was asleep I was wracked with insomnia and stress. I would try and plan the entire next day. I would write with a torch as my husband slept, meticulously documenting each feed. In five months, I lost twenty-five kilograms and was skeletal." Her life on the surface was carrying on as normal.

"I said all the right things, had family and friends around to dinner and tea. But inside I was like a wound-up coil. I had bald patches from ripping out my hair. I hated every second of breastfeeding and would be in a constant state of barely controlled panic."

> "There is just so long you can pretend you are okay before you crack."

HOW ARE YOU FEELING?

You could be depressed if these apply:

- You are irritable or confused.
- You feel like crying for no reason.
- You feel helpless, inadequate and unable to cope.
- You worry all the time.
- You feel scared and panicky.
- You feel ashamed and guilty.
- You don't know who you are any more.
- You have no interest in anything.
- You don't sleep the way you used to.
- You don't eat the way you used to.
- You don't love the baby the way you feel you should.
- You don't want sex any more.
- You sometimes think of hurting the baby or yourself.

Every new mother has felt one if not all of the symptoms listed above. So how do you draw the line and say it's PND and not the normal turmoil of motherhood? Ask yourself:

- Is it interfering with your daily functioning?
- Can you get to the shops, cook a meal, read a book or eat?

The Doc says that, when any of these everyday functions start slipping, you are dealing with pathology. "Everyone has felt anxious for a moment or an hour, but it did not stop them sleeping or eating. If symptoms persist for more than two weeks, you are dealing with something more than anxiety or loss of appetite."

THE EDINBURGH POST-NATAL DEPRESSION SCALE

These ten questions have been developed to help you diagnose whether you may be suffering from PND. Answer all ten questions, considering how you have been feeling for the past seven days, not just today. If you score higher than twelve, speak to your midwife, GP or gynae.

In the past seven days:

1. I have been able to see the funny side of things

As much as I always could	[0]
Not quite so much now	[1]
Definitely not so much now	[2]
Not at all	[3]

2. I have looked forward to things

As much as I ever did	[0]
Rather less than I used to	[1]
Definitely less than I used to	[2]
Hardly at all	[3]

3. I have blamed myself unnecessarily when things went wrong

Yes, most of the time	[3]
Yes, some of the time	[2]
Not very often	[1]
No, never	[0]

I had a fantasy that I was pushing my baby in the supermarket trolley and it started rolling down a hill, and I just let it roll away forever.

4. I have been anxious or worried for no very good reason

No, not at all	[0]
Hardly ever	[1]
Yes, sometimes	[2]
Yes, very often	[3]

5. I have felt scared or panicky for no very good reason

Yes, quite a lot	[3]
Yes, sometimes	[2]
No, not much	[1]
No, not at all	[0]

6. Things have been getting on top of me

Yes, most of the time	[3]
Yes, sometimes	[2]
No, not much	[1]
No, not at all	[0]

7. I have been so unhappy that I have had difficulty sleeping

Yes, most of the time	[3]
Yes, sometimes	[2]
No, not much	[1]
No, not at all	[0]

8. I have felt sad or miserable

Yes, most of the time	[3]
Yes, quite often	[2]
No, not much	[1]
No, not at all	[0]

9. I have been so unhappy that I have been crying

Yes, most of the time	[3]
Yes, quite often	[2]
Only occasionally	[1]
No, never	[0]

" I have never had feelings of: 'I hate my son', or 'I don't want my son' but I would get up and just know that I could not face the day."

10. The thought of harming myself has occurred to me

Yes, quite often   [3]

Sometimes   [2]

Hardly ever   [1]

Never   [0]

SCORE: [ ]

Taken from the British Journal of Psychiatry by J.L. Cox, J.M. Holden, R. Sagovsky (June 1987, Vol. 150)

LEVEL 1: THE BABY BLUES

Incidence: Ninety per cent of mothers.

Hits: Around the third day.

You feel: Overwhelmed, anxious, exhausted, weepy, inadequate, fearful, desperate, with nightmares, obsessive behaviour.

Lasts: Usually a day or two. Can drag on for a week.

Treatment: Sleep, support and time.

"Looking back now, it seems like such a small hurdle, like a bad bout of flu, but then it was all-consuming. At the time, I saw it as such a weakness, now I see it as such a strength, that I recognised it so fast, got help, and I got better."

LEVEL 2: POST-NATAL DEPRESSION

Incidence: Some fifteen to twenty per cent of new moms report PND, but the actual figures are thought to be much higher.

Hits: It may begin as early onset baby blues that just never go away or it may not appear until up to a year after the birth of the baby.

You feel: See the Edinburgh Post-natal Depression Scale on pg 170.

Lasts: From three months to decades, if not treated.

Treatment: Support, sleep, therapy and often antidepressant medication.

LEVEL 3: POSTPARTUM PSYCHOSIS

Incidence: One in a thousand.

Hits: During the first few weeks after birth.

Feels: On a scale of one to ten of irrational behaviour, you are hitting twenty. You are experiencing dramatic changes in behavior, feelings of being out of touch with reality, delusions of grandeur, memory loss, hallucinations and severe mood swings.

Lasts: The sooner it's treated, the sooner it ends.

Treatment: This is a medical emergency and needs immediate hospitalisation.

Why me?

Much of the medical controversy surrounding PND centres on the question of its cause. What actually causes this deep depression, and can it be avoided? Why do some women get it and not others? Is it random, or are there pre-existing conditions that make some women more susceptible to it? That is the clincher. And despite extensive research into PND, little has been proven. But theorists have put forward a number of trends that could influence your susceptibility to getting PND. (See who gets PND, pg 179.)

" Here's what I learned. Kids like happy mothers, so nurture your sense of self. Be selfish. Don't end up resenting your child. Do what you need to do to make yourself happy. If that means working, go and work. Make time for you. Don't feel guilty. Don't be stubborn. Don't be ashamed. Get help. "

MANIC PANIC

The most obvious cause is the massive and uncontrollable change in your life. This is a life-changing event and some women feel totally out of control, desperate and dangerous. Like any traumatic, or life-changing event, childbirth leaves many unscathed, but catches a few unsuspecting warriors in its nets. Libby was in her late fifties when she went on antidepressant drugs after the death of her husband.

"It was months later, when the depression had lifted, that I started to realise I had been depressed most of my adult life. I had always said my life changed after the birth of my first son, but what I never admitted was that I had been in a low-level depression ever since."

CAST ADRIFT

Many theorists believe that, in a Western environment, PND is a phenomenon that is worsened, if not caused, by the alienation young mothers experience. Women are isolated at home, left adrift with a new baby. Few of us have any experience of tiny babies. We have not witnessed the emotional and logistical challenges a small child presents, like rural and community-driven cultures have. In many parts of the world, the incidence of PND in traditional societies would appear to be low. These cultures, among other levels of support offered to a new mother, often provide a ritual transition period for new mothers and community support. Despite the strong rural culture in South Africa, it exhibits trends in keeping with a Western environment – perhaps exacerbated even by the urban-rural divide that often means babies are sent home to their rural grandparents as their mothers stay and work in the cities. A recent study in Khayelitsha by the University of Cape Town shows PND occurrence as high as

> **"** Society has eroded the importance of being a mother. Largely, I defined myself by what I'd been paid to do in the past. When this was replaced by a non-paying role, without recognition on completion of tasks, I felt worthless. **"**

thirty per cent, and this is attributed to the incidence of violence, abuse of alcohol and the experience of poverty.

In Japanese culture, the transition to motherhood begins at the wedding. A woman's role shifts so significantly to that of homemaker, that the transition to mother is smoother. In the Nigerian Yoruba tribe, the ritual transition starts when a woman moves into her third trimester of pregnancy. It is then that she moves back home with her mother and starts to prepare for her new role.

What do we do? We keep on pumping until the fortieth week and then start the countdown until our "normal lives" start again.

UNREALISTIC EXPECTATIONS

What we know of motherhood is from the mass media and air-brushed images of adoration. The worship of celebrities means the perma-tanned, calm and glamorous images of new mothers present an artificial norm of what it means to get our lives back. Catherine Zeta-Jones dropped thirty kilograms a few months after the birth of her daughter. Madonna had a stomach like an ironing board just weeks after the surgical birth of her daughter Lourdes. Super-organised Elle McPherson was glowing and gushing about bringing up her son Flynn with no nanny. She ran a successful international career alongside a small baby. Then she collapsed on the set of *Friends* and was hospitalised for exhaustion.

The lack of real information means there is a misrepresentation of what motherhood is about. It's depicted as glowing, healthy, desirable and manageable. It comes as a very real shock when it's none of those things to you.

"I was going to pop them out, take a few months off with each baby and get back to my life." Rita is a 32-year-old financier. "I had never heard a bad word said about motherhood. I thought if

" It took the almost irreparable breakdown of my marriage for me to seek counselling. I only went to appease the attorney. I did so under duress and with a negative attitude of mammoth proportions. "

Reese Witherspoon can do it at twenty, I can sure as sugar do it at thirty." But there she was, eight months later, sitting with a belly like a wobbly blancmange, massively oversized udders and a tiny tot that she had no control over. "I stumbled through each day with a smile fixed on my face. I had a nanny and a doting grandmother, but I was in a neurotic state of unbearable anxiety all day, fearing the second I got home and the long night alone with Alan. There was Catherine Zeta-Jones, who had Dylan round about the same time as me, squeezed into a size 10 gown and glowing. I was a failure."

It's a powerful illusion that all other women are simply loving motherhood and getting on with their lives and careers without a glitch. But it does look that way. You spot them with long strides on the treadmill and floating around with shiny hair and a wink that says, "I got it all this morning." And there you are, frazzled, neurotic, perpetually exhausted and considering assaulting a bank teller. Take heart that almost every new mom has taken a spot in that queue.

BRAIN DRAINED

Some experts believe that the body's inability to adjust to the different hormone levels after giving birth, affects the brain's neurotransmitters. It does seem likely that PND is related to the huge hormonal drop that takes place after the birth, but there is still

" *I was there alone hour after hour, week after week. I had visitors. But they would all leave, and I would be in this empty house with this tiny baby. I just did not know what to do with it. In desperation, I stage-managed bumping into my neighbour and struck up a friendship with her. I felt totally alone in the world and like it would never end.* "

no evidence to link it directly to hormonal changes. No real differences have been found during clinical trials between the hormonal changes of women who do, and do not, get PND. Some women though, are more susceptible to hormonal changes because they have hormone-sensitive brains. A telltale sign will be if you suffer from PMS. This is certainly a reaction to hormones.

A blood test for thyroid function is vital. Hypothyroidism (low or underactive thyroid function) has been linked to anhedonic depression while postpartum hyperthyroid (overactive thyroid function) is more prone to manifest as anxious depression. A drop in thyroid levels occurs naturally during the postpartum period. Your doctor will also rule out anaemia and iron deficiency.

All of these conditions can manifest as anxiety or a feeling of "flatness".

LOOKING GOOD

More and more women are choosing to have babies later in life once they have strong careers and definite ideas on how their life will run. The older childbearing age also leads to more compli-cations and challenges and, sometimes, longer physical recover-ies – you just don't look as good anymore. But even for many younger women, success means a sexy car, a big salary, a pow-erful job and looking damn fine. That's what we think for most of our lives. We don't measure success by what we are but by what we have. "That is," says Doc Andy, "until you have a baby."

"You are sitting at home alone with a needy, helpless baby who gives no acknowledgement back. While it is not quite as obvious or one-dimensional as that, a condition such as PND is going to require you to look fearlessly at who you are and on what you judge your self-worth.

" I think that part of why I got PND was that I planned so far in advance what I was going to do with this little baby. I would dress her up, take her out ... and when it actually happened, it was nothing like I had imagined. "

"My husband was the last to admit I had a problem. He kept saying: 'Stop saying its PND. If you keep saying it, you will end up creating it.' He would force me to get on my exercise clothes and go to gym, thinking it would somehow snap me out of it."

Defining your success by external yardsticks is something that has to change some time. Having a baby forces a change and fast."

Facing up to these changes can be daunting and create a total re-evaluation of yourself and your life.

BREAST TEST

Many mothers identify a strong link between their breastfeeding and their depression. This is not a result of the physiological act of nursing but the anxiety associated with breastfeeding and having to be available day and night to respond to your baby. Breastfeeding actually releases seratonin, which induces a feeling of wellbeing, but the stress of nursing, especially when you are experiencing pain and difficulties with the process, can be huge.

There is some evidence to support the opinion that nursing mothers are more prone to depression. In fact, hormones settle down more gradually when a mother breastfeeds. Doc Andy says that you will have a better response to the treatment of PND if you stop breastfeeding.

"Stopping breastfeeding will allow time for more sleep and a greater degree of support than you can allow when you are the sole supplier of your baby's nutritional needs. But this has to be a personal and informed choice you make.

Who gets PND?

Personality predisposition: You are organised, perfectionist, career-driven or in control. You may have elements of obsessive-compulsive behaviour around tidiness, making lists, cleanliness or work. Be warned. PND doesn't happen to wimps.

Behavioural or hormonal predisposition: You have a family history of any psychiatric condition, PND or panic disorders. You have bad PMT.

Environmental or life stress: Your reaction to the challenge of a small baby is influenced by your relationship, support system, family, financial security, previous loss of a family member or child and previous fertility problems. Moving home is a major stress.

REMEMBER:
You are not alone. Many women suffer this.
You are not to blame.
If you had any choice, you would not get this.
You will get well.

" I had no idea what was normal. Was it normal for a new mother to cry for ten hours a day? Was it normal to bite your nails until they bled? Was it normal to want to quietly just slip away from life? "

BAD MOMMY!

Are you not quite holding it together? Do you suspect that there are other moms out there who are struggling like you? Would you like to – Shock! Horror! – have a good laugh at it all? Fortunately, to keep us bad girls sane, there has been somewhat of a backlash against the super-serious advice and mega-moms who seem to cope with everything.

Writers are coming out of the closet and are letting other women know that perfect moms are all an illusion. Taking a slow cue from *Ab Fab's* notorious anti-mom Eddie, the Brits were the first off the block. The British website Bad Mothers Club has set a new standard for mothers who are prepared to stand up and say: "It sucks."

Columnist Stephanie Calman is the brains behind the site (www.badmothersclub.co.uk) that features articles such as "Boiled grey knickers", "Five essential childcare rules, and why you should break them" and "Why not to have hot sex".

British writer Allison Pearson blew the roof off the illusion that it's easy to work and have kids in her best-selling debut novel *I Don't Know How She Does It*. Her heroine is a top-notch but totally strung-out City fund manager who finds herself frantically bashing store-bought mince pies in the small hours of the morning so they look homemade for her child's school fete.

The Bitch in the House is an anthology of essays, collected by Cathi Hanauer, by high-powered American career girls who tell it like it is, some showing the thin line of tolerance and sanity they tread as mothers with careers. *The Mommy Myth: The idealization of motherhood and how it has undermined women* by Susan Douglas and Meredith Michaels has been making waves in the US by blowing the romantic notion of motherhood out of the water. The Bad Mom trend says let's stop pretending and get real. And it's a huge relief to find that other women share your feelings.

Get help: PND is a treatable condition with a very good prognosis. This may be a pre-existing condition. Having a baby has just triggered it and it, may never emerge again.

PND is:

- Predictable
- Common
- Treatable

What's the treatment?

ADMIT IT

There is no other time in your life that you are so exposed to health professionals as when you have given birth, yet PND goes unrecognised and misunderstood. Dr Andy looks at some of the reasons this happens:

- You have a self-judgement that you have failed at motherhood and that you will be judged for not coping while everyone else does, so you wear a mask to the outside world and continue to wear it until the wheels fall off. You even wear the mask to your husband.

- Women have an incredible capacity to endure pain and just keep going. You don't know when the balance has been tipped. You are confused, feeling out of control and everyone is telling you that's exactly what they felt. You convince yourself that this is normal, and it becomes tough to judge when it has gone beyond run-of-the-mill postpartum changes and into the realm of depression.

" At no point, could I intellectually see that this was a phase or that it would end. It was all-consuming, bottomless and endless. When I look back now, it seems small. But then, it was so huge."

"When my wife was diagnosed with PND, it was an incredible relief. I thought I had lost her, that childbirth had taken her away and left me with a total stranger in her place. The fact that she simply had a condition and that we were going to treat it, was like the answer to a prayer to me."

- Often, women who get PND are achievers and women in control of their lives. Admitting a problem is their first challenge. "Know that no mother would ever choose to get PND," says Doc Taub, "but you do have a choice with what you do with it."

"One of the toughest parts of treating PND is coming to terms with the fact that you are suffering from a clinical depression. It is so disappointing," says our doc. "It is not as you expected it to be."

The longer you leave it, the more stubborn the condition is. Don't wait two years. There are women who have never been treated, thirty years on. These women say things like: "I have never been the same again", or "I never got over it". You know better.

SUPPORT, SUPPORT, SUPPORT

This is the most critical aspect of the treatment. You need to get a support system in place to help you; your therapist or doctor will assist you in structuring a support team and calling in the troops. Doc Andy lays down the law on making yourself supportable.

"The first important thing to realise is that it's tough for you to be left alone with your child. This is not because you could harm it or do something wrong, far from it. It is because it is too scary for you to be alone with it. What often helps is someone simply

" I walked into my husband's study after three months of medication, looked at him and said: 'I'm back'. He broke down in wracking sobs. I had been so absorbed with my own recovery, I had not noticed he was close to breaking point. He had carried the family alone. I had left him alone. "

sitting with you at your house. This act must not disempower you. You need to handle your child, but you need the company and support a second person will bring. This means you need a roster of friends and family so you are never left alone. A nanny is not enough. You need someone who chats to you, keeps you going and simply passes the time with you."

"Next thing, your husband will be asked to attend a few sessions with you and your therapist. He too has been suffering from post-birth adjustment and it's an immense relief for many men to have a diagnosis and plan of action. He will be your first line of support. So he needs to understand your condition, your frame of mind and where he can best help. He needs to be guided in being the primary support person and educated in this decision. It may be the first time he has heard of it."

SUPPORT MEANS:
Saying: I do not judge you.
Asking: What do you need from me?
Listening: Not giving advice.

Therapy

There is a tough road to recovery, but your therapist will walk it with you. First, you need to get the basics right.

Dr Deborah Sichel recommends a five-level attack (NURSE) in her book *Woman's Moods*. (*Woman's Moods* by Deborah Sichel and Jeanne Watson Driscoli published by Quill 2000).

N Nutrition. Get your eating right.

U Understanding of the condition and yourself. Read up about your condition, speak to other women and know what's going on. Look at your own life, the decisions and judgments that have brought you here. Women who are prepared to look at themselves and get to know themselves will heal.

R Relaxation and rest. Rest. Rest. Rest. Rest.

S Spiritual knowing. Know that this is your journey.

E Exercise. Get moving. This is not debatable as it produces natural endorphins, our feel-good hormones.

If you have attended to all of the above and there is still no relief, your therapist will discuss the need for medication.

"I had no idea where to get help. My gynae just gave me the name of a psychiatrist who had a six-month waiting list. I called nine psychiatrists and they all gave me the same story. I was at a point where I could see I needed help, and I had no idea where to turn."

Medication

It's a huge adjustment to consider having to go on to medication, even for a gal who's consumed more recreational drugs than Courtney Love. There is a stigma attached to mental illness.

- Husbands apply a stigma. "You have a perfect child," they say. "How can you get depressed? I don't get it." (They will get it, says Dr Andy, because there is no choice. We like her.)
- You hold a judgement against yourself.

"Everyone else is coping, why not me?"

"I won't give my power away to a pill."

"I can do it myself."

- The medical profession applies a stigma. You won't be skimming over that section in the healthcare insurance questionnaire that asks if you have ever suffered a mental illness.

For most women who have been treated for PND, medication has been a lifeline back to normality. For some women, it is a last resort; for others, their first port of call. Speed is of the essence, to ensure that the relationship between you and your baby is affected for as little time as possible. Once they kick in, the benefits happen fast, but the two weeks until the medication works feels like an eternity for the mother. Severe depression is an unbearable space and hours seem like a lifetime. The effects of psychological treatments are not usually evident for weeks, or more often months, whereas interim drugs can start to relieve anxiety and insomnia symptoms within days. Don't be ashamed to use them to tide you over this very difficult time.

What's on the trolley tonight?

The usual medications used are antidepressant and antipsychotic drugs.

There are, in broad terms, five major groups of antidepressants:

- The tricyclic antidepressants (TCAs)
- The selective serotonin re-uptake inhibitors (SSRIs such as Zoloft or Prozac)
- The "newer" antidepressants (including mirtazapine, nafazodone and venlafaxine)

" I remember going to birthday parties. Mothers would be talking about the stages their kids were at from one month to two years. It would be teething problems or walking or talking. I would just sit with this feeling of sick dread. Like it is just never going to get better."

- Mood stabilisers (lamicten, lithium carbonate, quinolum)
- The monoamine oxidase inhibitors (MAOIs)

Eglanol (sulpiride) is one of the most commonly prescribed anti-depressants; so widely used among mothers, it's as common in bathroom cabinets as Rennies. In fact, it is not an antidepressant – it is an antipsychotic with antidepressant features and may work as treatment for postpartum depression. It is useful to stimulate lactation and happens to be a mild mood enhancer.

Eglanol aside, the first line of attack is usually an SSRI, and most commonly Prozac. SSRIs are for anxious depression, are incredibly effective and as popular as Disprin among suburban sets, where it's affectionately called Vitamin P. You need to know that they take two or three weeks to start making a difference. PND usually carries the associated symptoms of anxiety and insomnia; tackling these first provides some relief while you are waiting for the effects of the SSRI to kick in. The SSRI itself will then take care of anxiety and insomnia as well as start to tackle the underlying depression.

The rule of thumb is to stay on medication from six to twelve months.

By eight or nine months of treatment, you will feel like you are riding the crest of a wave. Then your doctor will start to tail off the medication within two or three months, although some doctors will recommend a longer tail-off of around four to six months, to reduce the chances of a relapse.

"I drove myself to a psychiatric facility and screamed at the gates to be let in. I thought about death non-stop and knew I would soon not be able to control my suicidal tendencies."

> *" I ran away from home for fourteen days. I just walked out on my two-year-old son, my twelve-week-old baby and my husband, without a second's thought. I drove for four hours and then checked into a guesthouse and watched TV for ten hours at a stretch. They did not enter my mind and I felt a detached bliss and an overwhelming desire to run from my life. "*

A little bit on the side

None of these drugs are without side effects and forewarned is forearmed. You need to know what you are in for and for the first four to six weeks many women feel a side effect more significantly than any improvement in their depression. The side effects can be debilitating and the choice is sticking it out or coping with the depression without medication.

Once you have passed six weeks, the lifting of the depression will ameliorate many negative symptoms.

If you are experiencing significant side effects, discuss this with your doctor. Do not feel tempted to simply stop the medication. You may try another medication. Should you be clear you want to stop, you will slowly reduce dosage under the guidance of your doctor.

"Isn't this a false high from the medication, and I will come crashing back into depression when I stop?"

No, says Doc Andy. "Medication is an intervention that is bringing you to normality, not giving you a false normality – just as a diabetic needs insulin to function normally or a person with high blood pressure needs medication. It's just that you may not need the medication forever."

However, stopping the medication can mean that you have a recurrence of the depression. That is why it is critical to treat PND on a number of levels. Medication is a tool. You need to

> *" I felt incredible pressure to have PND and was assured that the medical establishment would rush in with its drugs and take all the responsibility away from me. "*

tackle the underlying issues with therapy, self-discovery, time and ongoing medical monitoring.

What if the medication doesn't help?

The medication will bring some relief, but perhaps not the first drug you try. "What may happen is that the first drug you try may not suit you, and you may find its side effects unbearable," Doc Andy says. Even then, your anxiety and insomnia can be treated, which is a significant step in the right direction. Then your doctor will start finding an antidepressant that works more effectively for you. Either you will increase the dosage, add complementary medication or switch to something else.

Relax, this condition can be treated effectively.

"Another option is electroconvulsive therapy (ECT) which, although it may sound alarming, is extremely effective in severe depression and may be life-saving. Severe depression is when you start having suicidal tendencies or thoughts of hurting the baby," says Doc Andy.

"I was fine most of the day, but by five every day, I had hit a brick wall. The tears would start flowing. I felt I could not go on, I could not face another endless night alone in the nursery."

How will PND affect my baby?

Long-term studies in babies show possible cognitive and behavioural disturbances in children of depressed mothers, but be assured that this happens only if the depression is not treated for a longer period of time. This time is regarded as three months. This means the sooner you get help, the better it is for you and your family.

Firstly, you need to accept that you are not going to bond with your baby while you have PND. Relax about it. There is no rule that says if you do not feel gushing love by five months, you are never going to. Bonding is rarely immediate and most mothers say they only started to relate to their babies as anything other than dependant little leeches after six months, when they started to respond to things.

"You have a lifetime to bond," says Doc Andy. "There is another parent to bond with your baby for now. Stop trying to do everything."

Until recently, Prozac was deemed the safest drug for pregnancy and it was the only approved drug in pregnancy. But now there are warnings that it is not entirely safe for pregnant women – some recent trials show a lower birth weight in babies exposed to the drug in utero. While some studies have shown that there are possible risks to the child when the mother takes Prozac, one must remember that a mother's mental health is also important to the child. All antidepressants are secreted in breast milk and the same rules of drug taking apply as during your pregnancy. The limited clinical trials show that the concentrations are low, to the point of being barely detectable. Nonetheless, many mothers choose to stop breastfeeding to eliminate any risk of transmission. The decision is yours, make an informed one.

If you continue to breastfeed:
- Time your dose so that you take it before your baby's longest sleep.
- Breastfeed immediately before you take your medication.
- Express a few ounces before you feed as medication tends to sit in your foremilk.
- Discuss with your doctor taking your medication as a single dose, rather than spreading it over the day.

" I walked into the clinic in midwinter in shorts, slipslops and a vest, screaming that they should lock me up. It took four orderlies to restrain me from climbing into a hospital bed. "

- Consider a bottle for the closest feed and then breast.
- Avoid nursing for two to three hours after taking a dose.

Hormone treatment

Many women prefer to try hormone treatment, rather than anti-depressants, because they see it as more natural and may feel they have had good results from hormone treatment. Many doctors don't rate it, but it's worth a shot. Progesterone is best as a suppository or cream, while oestrogen is sometimes applied in skin patches.

Natural support

Drink tea: Drink calming teas, at least four cups a day: chamomile, rosehip, hops, vervain, wild lettuce, passion flower and lemon verbena.

Homeopathy: Saint John's wort (hypericum): It is widely used to help combat mild to moderate depression. Note that Saint John's wort affects the efficacy of the Pill so be warned if you want to wait for your second child.

"I resisted Prozac for six months. I felt a failure. I had two healthy boys; a fabulous life and I needed drugs to make me happy! Eventually, I knew I needed help."

Gelsemium 30c and Argentum nitricum: These are often considered for symptoms of anxiety, sense of imbalance, apprehension and panic.

Aconitum napellus: This is useful in combating pressing anxiety and panic attacks.

Supplements: B-complex, folic acid and Omega 3 fatty acids are highly recommended for help with depression and are best taken in the form of flaxseed oil.

Avoid: Ceylon tea, coffee, alcohol and sugar, as they worsen anxiety.

Exercise: Aim for four or five times a week for forty minutes at a time. The release of beta-endorphins will pick you up.

Massage: This is proven to reduce cortisol – the natural stress hormone.

Will it happen again?

It can. You have uncovered a pre-existing condition and have treated it effectively, but it can appear again. You will be carefully monitored if you have a second pregnancy and may be put on antidepressants at around eight months to prevent a relapse.

WHAT DO I DO?

Call the Post-Natal Depression Support Association (PNDSA) on 021 797 4498 or 083 309 3960 or 082 882 0072.
Email PNDSA secretary Colleen Knutsen: colleen@pndsa.co.za

- www.pndsa.co.za
- Go to your GP who will refer you to a specialist for treatment.
- Call the Anxiety and Depression Support Group on 011 783 1474, or visit their website: www.anxiety.org
- Visit the Postpartum Support International website, which includes a special section for new fathers: www.postpartum.net

KNOW THE EXPERTS

PSYCHIATRISTS

Training: MBChB or MBBCh degree and four years of specialisation, a total of twelve years of study. They are qualified medical doctors who specialise in psychiatric conditions. They deal with a range of mental problems, such as bipolar disorders, eating conditions and phobias.

Technique: Prescribe medication or engage in psychotherapy.

Cost: Medical aid rates are R93 for twenty minutes or R226 for an hour. Sixty per cent of practitioners charge private rates which vary at around R390 for half an hour and R590 for an hour.

Contact: SA Society of Psychiatry on 021 557 9373 or www.sasop.co.za

PSYCHOLOGISTS

Training: BA or BSc in psychology and a Masters degree. They deal with a patient's emotional wellbeing, including obsessive-compulsive disorders, eating disorders, anxiety and depression. They cannot prescribe drugs.

Technique: Work through therapeutic methods such as talk therapy, hypnosis and play therapy.

Cost: Medical aid rates are R93 for twenty minutes or R226 for an hour. Most are in private practice and charge more.

Contact: Psychological Society of SA on 011 486 3322 or www.psyssa.com

Check what your medical aid will cover. You foot the bill over the above rates.

Ask for a treatment plan, this cannot go on endlessly, and know how many sessions you need before you see results. If there is not a significant improvement after four sessions, discuss this with your therapist.

DADS DEALING
WITH DEPRESSION

Your husband needs to know a few things:

■ Post-natal depression is treatable.

■ You will get the wife that you remember back.

■ You will have a healthy, perhaps better, marriage again.

■ Most women who have recovered say it's the best thing that ever happened to them because of the work that they've needed to do on themselves.

■ Motherhood is the most undervalued job. You need to walk through the door once a week and say to your wife: "You are remarkable."

■ PND offers the dad an opportunity to bond with the baby that he might not otherwise have had.

my story: Sharon

I woke up on Tuesday morning of week three and David was crying. He cried for about two hours at a time and then stopped to feed. On Wednesday, he cried for twelve hours with barely a stop. His night nurse arrived at 6pm and settled him almost immediately. When she left at 6am, he started up again. He cried and cried and cried and cried. It was colic, everyone agreed. I took him to a paediatrician on week four who confirmed what everyone had said. Colic.

Over the next two weeks, I was still myself. I was a competent investment banker trying to find solutions for a difficult situation. I tried everything.

I was sick with anxiety. When the day broke, I would wake up with a feeling of dread and fear and nausea. Monday was the worst day of the week, because the night nurse would be off, and there would be no end to the crying. I would dread Monday the whole week. I could not eat a morsel. I could not even find the will to buy food for the house. By week six, I was below my pre-pregnancy weight and falling fast.

I thought this was normal; this is what all mothers go through. All my friends had told me the first few months would be tough, but they got through it. So I couldn't help thinking: Why am I not coping? What is wrong with me? How come everyone else gets through this and I am breaking down?

On week seven, my in-laws came to visit, and I was open about the fact that I was not coping. I was open with everyone about it. They suggested that I get a day nurse as well as a night nurse. I now had someone looking after my baby day and night and I was living in an endless thick black funk.

I woke in week eight and could not get out of bed. Fortunately, I had seen this happen to my sister and suddenly knew it was PND. After countless calls and favours, I got a reference to a GP who specialised in PND. I called her and she said: "I can see you tomorrow. Can you wait that long?"

My visit with her was the beginning of my slow recovery. She put me on antidepressants and anti-anxiety medication immediately and warned me that it would get worse before it got better. By four and a half months, things started to lift and by six months, I felt significantly better, enough to return to work. Now I am better than I have ever been in my life.

It is the best thing that ever happened to me. I have been to the bottom and it's not that bad.

my story: Christine

The smell of breast milk turns my stomach. Some days I spend hours in the bath escaping the stench of soggy breast pads. The birth experience disgusts me. I have difficulty believing I'm a mother. I resign myself to getting used to it because there's no way it's going back where it came from.

Every night I go to bed and promise myself: "Tomorrow, I will stop this. Tomorrow will be different." When I crawl back into bed, I renew the worn-out promise and hate myself a little more. The baby cries and so do I.

A knock on the door is the worst thing that can happen in my day.

"Hi. How are you?"

"Absolutely crap! This baby terrifies me. I hate the way I look. I'm exhausted. I can barely remember my name. I don't feel a scrap of the motherly love everyone else gushes about. I think I'm losing my mind. Please help me."

Instead I sit by the crib, staring at the baby, willing him not to make a sound.

I live in Johannesburg. I have a helper who takes care of everything. So, what is it I do all day? There's no excuse for me to be tired all the time. I have a roof over my head, food in the fridge. My life is easy. I don't have half the issues many mothers around the world, or just down the road for that matter, have to deal with. My husband works in Cape Town, Monday to Thursday, so I don't even have him to worry about. I should be grateful.

My baby is ten months old when I find I am pregnant again. I don't like the baby I have. I don't like the mother I turned out to be. I loathe my husband. I'll tell him when we divorce that he can have custody of our child. It would be best for the baby. I know I am not a good mother.

I didn't know that I was depressed. I don't like failing, and that's how I saw it. Failing at the most natural task in the world. It's hardly as though I was trailblazing. You don't see women in the rice paddies or the refugee camps crying into their wicker baskets and rushing off for counselling. I felt like a spoilt brat. Billions of others coped. I must too.

my story: Diolinda

I had a traumatic birth with my first son. I had an emergency C-section and got a secondary infection that was agonising. Added to that, I had a reaction to the spinal block and was totally paralysed for a full day. I was kept in hospital for eight days, was emotional, distraught, in intense pain from the infection and could not sleep. It was in the hospital that I nearly lost my mind. My obstetrician would ask all these questions I knew were leading up to whether I was depressed or not. Sure I felt like crying all day, but I knew that it was frustration from my circumstances, self-judgement and hormones. Every conversation started with lines like: "You must remember that this depression is not your fault," or "How's your appetite?" My husband was even convinced that I was just in denial, and I often saw the obstetrician talking to him, after visiting me. I felt like I could be the only sane person in a loony bin. It was assumed that I must have PND after my complications and that I need only admit it, and I would be fixed with medication.

I was visited by endless nurses, the hospital social worker and sales people offering baby products – from photos to breastfeeding consultations. I never had a moment to just rest and bond. I was visited by a staff counsellor who ticked me off on a chart that described my moods, and told me I was depressed, but it could be fixed.

If I did not have a stronger sense of self, or a good sense of humour, I might have bought into the expectation that I needed help – and that that entailed drugs.

My poor husband was floundering and worried. He flew my mom out from the UK a week early to help me. When she arrived, I checked myself out of the clinic and got home. I felt fine. Sure I was weepy for a few weeks. I had moments of anxiety, paranoia, nightmares and all sorts of crazy thoughts. But I knew that this was just the everyday run of the emotional turmoil of having a tiny baby, and I wasn't going to allow a drug to dull the experience for me.

FROM LUSH *to* THRUSH: SEX AFTER THE STRETCH

Cosmo girls have sizzling sex. They scorch up the sheets and drive their men to distraction with ticklers and little finger tricks. They do things like lick their lips seductively, answer the door in French knickers holding a bowl of whipped cream and disappear under the bistro table, with a pat of butter.

Intimidating for the rest of us, who schedule the event a few days ahead and inevitably either forget or sleep through the Sunday morning sex date.

We must remember: Cosmo girls are eighteen, wear a size 6 and do not have babies. But women's magazines are where most of us learned about sex – how to do it better, how to wrap our legs around our ears like a pretzel and how to go multiple. It's also how we all like to think we are in bed. And that may be true – for the first six months of a relationship.

Despite all the advice out there, there's a small gap in the market about how to keep a sizzling sex life going fifteen years and three children later. In fact, forget sizzling, any sex at all will do. And don't be fooled into thinking it only drops off after three kids. Even just the one can take up all your energy and time: all of a sudden you realise that the last time you had sex was after seven Kir Royales at Aunt Tilly's sixtieth … and that was six months ago.

CHAPTER 9

THAT KIND OF ADVICE REMAINS IN A DIFFERENT SEC-TION ALTOGETHER – advice columns on sexual problems or pamphlets in the doctor's waiting room. The fact that boredom, lack of libido and an end to sex remain on the letters pages perpetuates the myth that good sex is something that just happens and no sex means you are abnormal or have a problem. Well, that may be true of the first few years in a relationship, but it's only the exceptional couple who doesn't have to work harder than Britney Spears to stay on top.

Sex may have got you into a relationship. It may have kept you going until that first child arrives, but after that, the two of you are going to have to work just to keep it going.

Sex is no longer spontaneous. Much like your relationship, it's not going to happen unless you do something about it.

Couples aren't warned about all this. You're totally unprepared for the knock your sex life will take once your baby has arrived.

Most couples, understandably, believe that once the baby is born, their life will go right back to how it was pre-pregnancy. In fact, many men count down the days during the last few months to the return of regular sex. In the first few weeks, the delusion may persist as you are both enveloped in a hormonal love cocoon that will see you packing in some fast and creative action (although you don't even have time to floss). But the cold reality will set in fast. You are exhausted, sleep-deprived, anxious, angry, frustrated, stressed, and, as the mom, also bleeding, sore and large.

You do not want sex.

Welcome to parenting, where what you thought is not what you get.

Let's get the facts out of the way first:

> *"Somehow I was pregnant again, six months later. I would swear you had to have sex to conceive, and it seemed like we never got it together."*

Doc's endorsement

You doctor will tell you to wait six weeks, to be certain all is in the clear. But in reality, few couples wait that long. Your body is flooded with oxytocin, "the hormone of love", and you may want a bit of lovin' to go with it.

The primary concern is infection, not pain. Your body is still incredibly vulnerable to infection, and the last thing you want to contend with is a complication at this point. If you were going to cut it fine, week two would be acceptable. By the second week normal episiotomy stitches and lacerations have largely healed and your cervix has closed. Bruising and swelling will have gone down significantly.

If you experienced any complications or concerns during your birth – any severe lacerations or cuts, haemorrhage or significant blood loss – you are definitely going to have to wait six weeks before you get the go-ahead.

C-section delivery means you have escaped all stress to your vagina and just have to watch out for general infection and cleanliness.

As a rule of thumb, you should wait until the heavy red bleeding has stopped.

Be sensible. If you feel pain, stop. You have not had an internal examination and you could have something a bit out of place. It would be unforgivably silly to cause damage to yourself for a few minutes of fun.

Use your imagination. Sex is not only about penetration! Some possibilities include sexy stares across the room, dirty talk, sensual massage, showering or bathing together, mutual masturbation or anything else in between.

" We get undressed, look at each other fondly over the pillows and say: Goodnight. "

FROM LUSH *to* THRUSH: SEX AFTER THE STRETCH

Fear factor: contraception

Although breastfeeding releases a hormone, prolactin, that helps suppress ovulation, you are a brave woman if you count only on breastfeeding for contraception. Nothing could be more terrifying that the thought of another pregnancy when you are battling with endless 24 hour cycles of feeding and burping. And yet, it happens. Not to us sassy girls who do our research, of course. But it does happen.

Those who rely on breastfeeding to keep the swimmers in check are following a method called lactational amenorrhoea method or LAM. This is a system, developed in 1988, by a group of scientists who met in Bellagio, Italy to define a set of guidelines that a woman could use to predict her fertility while breastfeeding. They concluded that exclusive breastfeeding could provide up to ninety-eight per cent effective contraception, if three criteria are met:

- Your periods have not resumed. (Bleeding up to the fifty-sixth postpartum day is considered part of the postpartum recovery process and is not counted as menstrual bleeding.)
- You are fully, or nearly fully, breastfeeding. This means you are supplementing no more than fifteen per cent of all feeds with any other liquid – goat's milk, formula, water or special supplements.
- The baby is less than six months old.

" On a scale of desire from one to ten, I am sitting on a minus eight. I have been there for two years, despite a few mercy bonks. "

Now we like the idea that this is ninety-eight per cent effective, but we don't want to be one of the two per cent who slip through the gap. This is why most obstetricians will recommend you supplement with additional birth control methods, such as condoms or a progesterone-only pill. (Combined oestrogen-progestogen pills can interfere with breastfeeding).

> *" It took about two years for us to restart a sex life. Neither of us wanted sex for a long time, it was never one-sided. Then slowly we started to reintroduce the sensuality in our relationship. "*

Do not use the return of your period as a gauge of your fertility. Don't forget that you ovulate and are fertile some fourteen days before you bleed, plenty of time for a sneaky fertilisation to take place, and you will be none the wiser for some time. Women who don't breastfeed usually find their menstrual cycle returns to normal rapidly – within about four to six weeks, but fertility can return from the second week postpartum.

Are breasts only for baby?

Certainly not; although your husband may have a little trouble regarding them as sexual objects while they are leaking milk and strapped in a fleshtone cotton feeding bra around the clock.

There is a bizarre contradiction going on in your relationship already. Your breasts belong to your baby right now and that's a strange concept for both of you. Your husband is probably as familiar with your breasts as you are and they are looking mighty fine and full right now. But they have a little mouth attached and that's quite a change.

Whether it's jealousy or curiosity that spurs it, there'll be a bigger mouth attached at some time. If there is a husband in the house who says he has not sampled breast milk, there is only one response: Liar.

As long as you are comfortable with it, go ahead. He is not going to deprive your child of nutrition.

FROM LUSH *to* THRUSH: SEX AFTER THE STRETCH

PROTECTION TABLE

THE PILL

If you are bottle-feeding you can go back on your old method of contraception. But breastfeeding mothers need to consult their obstetricians and will usually be placed on a progestogen-only pill, aka the Mini Pill. Combined oestrogen-progestogen pills can interfere with breastfeeding.

99.9 per cent effective

CONDOMS

This latex device has a bad rep, as men moan about loss of sensation, but this is still the contraception of choice for many women as you avoid the side effects that can be associated with other methods. One way that your husband can improve his sensitivity is to practise by masturbating while wearing a condom. If you have postpartum vaginal dryness, you will need to make liberal use of a water-based lubricant during sex.

ninety per cent effective

THE INJECTION

You will be nabbed with a quarterly injection of progesterone that will suppress ovulation. If you are thinking of a second baby, give this option a skip as the hormone lingers in your system. It takes six to nine months before you are fertile again.

99.7 per cent effective

IUDS

Intrauterine devices have come a long way since they were a coiled loop or a copper-T. The most commonly used brand is Mirena. This only needs replacing every five years and is fitted by your obstetrician. It slowly secretes a hormone called levonorgestrel into your womb, where it thickens the mucus and thins the lining of the womb, to prevent eggs implanting. Extremely effective in treating heavy periods.

ninety-eight per cent effective

THE PATCH

This option has been approved in the US and should be available in South Africa soon. A patch dispensing both oestrogen and progestogen is applied to your stomach, butt or arm. You slap a new one on once a week and go patch-free for the fourth week (much the like the placebo pills in the Pill). If you're not breastfeeding, you can go on the patch as early as four weeks after delivery. As with other methods, ask your physician for a prescription. It's not recommended for breastfeeding women.

ninety-nine per cent effective

Gushing desire

Since the same hormone, oxytocin, released during sex also causes your milk to eject, do not be surprised if you are suddenly spouting fountains of milk from your breasts as you get aroused. It can be a bit of a shock but it's usually hilarious. The best way to get around this is to nurse before you are planning any action.

GETTING HOT WHILE NURSING

I had an incredibly powerful feeling, that all my insides were moving when I breastfed. Except the movement wasn't arousal – I wanted a bowel movement. Not exactly common, said my midwife. But then I've never really wanted to be common.

The vast majority of women feel lots of unusual things while breastfeeding – but very few actually feel aroused. Although it's rare, it's not impossible. Nipples may sit on the crest of your breast but they are the starting point of far more. During sex, stimulation of your nipples can be intensely arousing, causing sensations that shoot down your stomach and into your groin. Having a small baby attached to your nipple is also going to spark an awareness of feelings in your body you may not have felt before. There is nothing sexual about breastfeeding, so don't feel guilty about arousal. It's not as though you are finding your baby appealing, nor does it mean there is anything physically or

" My daughter never slept. Eventually, we just ended up having sex with her in the room, after numerous discussions on whether she would actually know what was going on. Then one morning, she actually climbed on Chris's back as it was rising and falling above me – that put an end to that. "

> *"My libido has been incredibly high. It started about four months after the birth. I feel aroused all the time, as if some muscles have been awakened deep inside me and I can't switch them off."*

emotionally wrong with you. It's a hormonal release. Both nursing and sex depend on increased levels of oxytocin, a hormone that also triggers the milk letdown reflex. The hormone also stimulates your need for physical touch.

To think that a baby may become aroused is obviously utter nonsense. Of course, breastfeeding feels lovely and comforting to a baby, but there is no correlation with a sexual feeling.

Most women feel a huge amount of satisfaction and an intense intimacy from breastfeeding. It is a tragedy if you equate that with anything improper.

DOES NURSING DROP MY LIBIDO?

Again, there is no easy answer here. Hormonally there is a lot going on while you breastfeed. Nursing increases two hormones, oxytocin and prolactin. The former is associated with sexual arousal and orgasm, while prolactin suppresses sexual desire and lowers testosterone – the hormone that fuels your libido.

In addition, breastfeeding means you are exhausted most of the time with ongoing nightly wakings and endless daily routines of feeding. Nothing kills a libido faster than exhaustion.

Other breastfeeding moms have a strong desire for sex. There is no right or wrong here. Sexual desire is more than the sum of its parts and each of us is different.

FROM LUSH *to* THRUSH: SEX AFTER THE STRETCH

WHEN SEX STOPS

Cosmo doesn't quite cover this territory and it's certainly not a topic to be discussed over a family dinner. Yet it's a familiar place for most couples (except Pamela Anderson who was cavorting on a swing above lucky Tommy Lee).

There are times, in every relationship, when sex comes to a dead end.

What makes a relationship grow and continue is the ability to work through these problems.

There will be many times like this, but one of the largest and most challenging shifts in your sexual relationship comes when you have children.

Sex is the last thing on your mind. You are busy, stressed and feel the size of a walrus and about as attractive.

Conservative research studies show that most couples have sex about sixty-one times a year, or slightly more than once a week. This figure is taken as an average across age groups. More internationally accepted averages put it at 2.5 times a week.

When does it become a problem?

"My wife is happy to have sex while he is crawling around on the floor, but I find it incredibly distracting and off-putting. But we virtually have no time alone. "

As soon as either of you think it is. Relationships can go for months without sex without either of you noticing. Bear in mind that the average is 2.5 times a week.

You are not housemates, nor are you aging aunties. You are young, fit and I am going to put my head on the block and say that if you have gone four months with no sexual contact, you are facing a bit of a problem you need to tackle head on.

Sex is a habit. It's easy to fall into a pattern of forgetting about it. But it's also easy to get back into regular sessions.

What is stopping you?

Your sex drive is more than the sum of its parts. It is neither wholly physical nor completely emotional. It's a complex, chemical relationship that merges hormones, fantasy and time with self-esteem, self-confidence and self-respect.

You may be one of the lucky few couples who have a chemistry you can't switch off. But if you are among the rest of the population, you are going to have to make time to rediscover your sex life.

There are two basic areas where problems could be affecting your desire: Your body and your mind.

Body

First up, you need to get the physical causes of libido loss sorted out.

YOUR BODY
You are healing and feel like hell. This is no time you want to climb on top of your husband wearing a cowboy hat and ride the rodeo. Give yourself time to heal and gather strength. No need to put pressure on yourself to perform in the sack when your first priority is to look after yourself and your own recovery.

CHECK YOUR PILLS
A notorious side effect of the ever-popular selective serotonin reuptake inhibitors (SSRIs, most notably Prozac or Paxil) is a lower libido and impaired orgasm. These are two of the most commonly prescribed antidepressants. Speak to your doctor about lowering your dosage.

Other medication that can impact libido are birth control pills,

" My husband is unresponsive. He is always too tired and fobs me off with a peck on the cheek. I feel rejected, unattractive and undesirable. "

blood pressure lowering drugs and, in some cases, oestrogen replacement. Consult your doctor if you suspect any of these are impacting on your sex life.

UNDERLYING DISORDERS

Medical complaints can knock your libido. These include thyroid deficiency, pain-causing urogenital problems such as fibroids, endometriosis, candida and bladder infections, vulvodynia or inflammation.

PAIN

Causes of pain fall into two categories.

Scarring: Perineal scarring heals fast, but women report itchiness and pain, sometimes for years after the event. The first priority here is to heal your wound, so don't rush into sex. If pain persists during sex after twelve months, check in with your obstetrician.

Penetration pain: This is a pain, or uncomfortable feeling, in the vagina during sex. Often it feels as if your partner's penis is too deep. The most common cause is early uterine descent. This means your uterus has dropped a few centimeters from its usual resting place and your partner's penis is hitting against your cervix during penetration. Another reason could be a prolapse of bladder or rectum. This would feel more like fullness in your bladder or rectum during sex.

"My wife allows our daughter to stay up until nine, when she is clearly ready for bed. I want her in bed by six, so we have the evening together and I do this when it's my chance. We fight about it continually. I don't want to lose my time with my wife, but she can't set down rules for her time with me."

"We are both so tired at night that we started this game, having sex in the garden shed during the kids' weekend nap. It's become our sanctuary and an incredibly secret space that only we share – the only secret space we have left!"

The first thing to do is to experiment and find a sexual position that eases the pressure.

The missionary, or any position where you are lying on your back with your legs pressed against your body will shorten your vaginal canal and cause additional pain. With you on top, you can control how far you are penetrated, or try a spooning position, which may ease the feeling of depth.

See Chapters 2 and 3 for ways to strengthen your uterine muscles and deal with prolapse.

DRY AS A BONE

Breastfeeding lowers levels of estradial, the hormone responsible for keeping the urogenital tract lubricated and supple. The symptoms will vary. This is temporary. Just stock up on some lubricating creams, oils or gels. Remember to use a water-based lubricant with condoms.

EXHAUSTION

This is a libido killer. Both of you are exhausted and sleep-deprived. Your lives are hectic, and when you fall into bed every night, sex is simply not on the agenda. Mornings are better.

STRESS

Having a child is stressful, compounded with money concerns, work stress, moving house, restarting work. When you are stressed, your libido is one of the first casualties.

Sure motherhood is stressful. But how long are you going to keep on trying to do everything? Find ways to limit the workload on yourself and reduce your most immediate stress.

Remember, it takes two to tango and two to raise the result of it.

Set rules for handling the baby, and make sure your partner shows up for his turn, even it's just handling the bath every day; take that time to walk away from your baby for a while.

Try and relax as a couple. It is easy to spend your precious time alone discussing your baby or just catching up on some sleep. But try and schedule some time to unwind together. Even if it's a stroll after dinner or a quick back massage before bed. Start to reconnect as a couple in a situation that does not include your baby.

Mind and soul

Yes, we know you just don't feel like it, but you need to look a bit deeper than that. Sex was part of your relationship before your baby; you need to look at what in you has changed.

DEPRESSION
Depression will hit your sex life hard, fast and first. Tackle the depression, and then work on getting your libido back.

> **"** *I was just staring at this mass of flesh in horror. My torso was twisted around and there were three rolls of fat, just spreading out beside me. My husband loved every minute, but I was in a state of extreme embarrassment. I could not wait for it to be over so I could cover up all that fat.* **"**

PERCEPTIONS OF YOUR BODY

A negative self-image can dampen even the most powerful sex drive. Nobody wants to do a striptease with a postpartum body. It would be more suited to a comedy routine. But chances are your husband thinks you are looking glorious and is glowing with love and pride. Try not to make your negative image his reality by suggesting he may find you anything other than a domestic goddess. Rather than feel exposed and uncomfortable, opt for some flattering and flowing lingerie that covers the bits you hate.

ANGER

Repressed emotions, such as anger, frustration and resentment, do not create a sizzle at night. Not unless you want to don latex and crack the whip. Chapter 11 deals with ways to clear the anger in your relationship without taking it out on each other.

SERIOUS MOM

Are you trying too hard to be a mommy? Sure you're a mommy. But you are also a daughter, sister, lover and friend to many people. Don't get too tied into being old before your time. Have fun with being a parent, for heaven's sake; don't make it a chore that swallows the rest of your life.

LAZINESS

It's very easy to let your sex life slide into a wasteland. Keeping the spice means hard work. Otherwise be prepared to be nothing more than very good friends.

"I cannot face my body. I lock the door when I bath and change in the bathroom. There is no way I am showing this strange thing off to my husband. He will have to wait. "

FROM LUSH *to* THRUSH: SEX AFTER THE STRETCH

It takes two to tango

Postpartum libido loss is by no means confined to women. There is a perception out there that men are gagging to get back into the sack and it's the women who are tired, listless and more into their books. This is not always the case. The stress of having a family is shared between partners. More often that not, your husband has taken up the slack while you are off work and is working 24/7 to compensate for the loss in income. Added to that is the responsibility of having a family, lack of spontaneity that a baby imposes on your life and emotional exhaustion. "My wife is making a real effort to restart our sex life, but I am totally without drive right now," says 32-year-old architect, Simon. "It inevitably turns into a dreadful scene and fuels all her insecurities about her body and desirability to me. But it's just that I am dog-tired and would rather sleep."

YOU ARE LOVERS
NOT HOUSEMATES

- Sex requires work.
- Get the kids to bed.
- Sex is not just about penetration.
- Just because you are not in the mood, doesn't mean you can't get there.
- You are not a performing seal. Have fun, add some games, but you do not have to resort to a high-wire act to get him fired up.

Dirty slapper

Slap on a blue movie: it will kick-start even the most sluggish motor.

Candles and lashings of fake tan: Candlelight is flattering
and brown fat looks sexier than white fat.

Anticipation works. Send an email: "I will be home at
seven. I expect to find you naked on the bed with a blindfold and
an iced bottle of schnapps."

Offer oral: Few men will refuse.

Sexy texts: Keep the fire burning with some X-rated SMS messages during meetings.

Handcuffs on the bed: You may not get to use them but the
sight of them will stoke even the coldest fire.

Get yourself fired up

Why are you waiting for your partner to put the vooma back into
your sex life?

There are three dynamics here. Your libido, his libido and the
times you connect.

You are responsible for your own libido and pleasure. You need
to show up for yourself first.

*" My wife lost her shape with our second child and eight years on, she has still made no
effort to lose the weight. I cannot broach it with her, but I am simply not attracted to the
flabby body she now wears. She used to be fit and toned. Our sex life never recovered and
it's taking its toll on our marriage. "*

WORK IT, GIRL

Get the kid to sleep: This is the first rule of saving your sex life. Nighttime is your time. The kid has had your day. Give the evening to yourself and sometimes your relationship. Bedtime is not a negotiable item on the menu.

Open up: It's hugely intimidating to simply be shrugged off when you initiate contact. Eventually, you will stop doing it. You owe it to your partner to share with them your feelings of exhaustion, your lack of physical confidence, your self-loathing or your numbness.

Own it: Don't make it about the other person. You are the one who doesn't feel like sex.

Do things together: Have a morning date at the gym; have a standing Sunday breakfast date and offload the baby at a friend first; do yoga together; find out about courses you can do together (massage, breathing, meditation). Jonti Searl's *Expanded Orgasm Workshops* are converting straight-laced lads into tantric tyrants (see Chapter 12 for details).

Turn off the telly: The only adult time you are going to have is after hours when the baby is asleep. Do something – don't sit gawping at the box.

Self service: There is little worse than a mercy shag. If you do not feel like it, tell him so and invite him to masturbate. Better still, you can certainly give him pleasure with a little lip or hand action if you are up for it.

Here are five ways to put a tired breeder on top form.

Buy some erotica: Women are turned on by erotic fiction and fantasy. Your imagination is lacking, so pop into a sex shop or second hand bookstore and stock up on some saucy tales. Some romance titles have some rauchy imprints if grabbing a *Taboo* is too much for you. Amazon.com brings a new level of anonymity to shopping.

Get in touch: Touch yourself. Just spend some time each day getting to know your body again. Grab a bottle of massage oil and vigorously rub it into your body in long, sweeping strokes. Get your circulation going and feel what it's like to have hot hands on your tush, even if they are yours. Take time to massage your head and feet.

Get active: Chose an exercise activity that pushes you to feel physical and complement it with something like yoga, which allows you to start to get in touch with your body. It's your responsibility to feel good about your body.

Fantasise: Time out is not time to worry about baby or to read another book on weaning. Get your sensual juices flowing. Lie back in a hot bath and imagine you are English rose, Sophia. A band of ruthless desert warriors has captured you and they want you as their bound and gagged sex slave.

Look fantastic: There is nothing like some sexy underwear to get you feeling hot. Suspender belts, lacy teddies and sheer bras don't only belong on soap operas.

" I am just so exhausted all the time. I feel so much has changed between us, that I battle to just let go of our rows, harsh words and stresses and just have good sex. It inevitably ends in a row. "

LICK YER LIPS, YOU LUSH

It's time to get off the notion that sex equals penetration. There are countless intimate acts that are sensual, unbearably sexy and do not involve intercourse. They just involve a little imagination.

Mind games: Think talking dirty is only something Colin Farrell does after a few whiskies? Not true. There is no need to act like a porn star and throw in every swear word you know – especially if it's totally out of character. No, it's much more effective if you use erotic language that describes how your body is responding and what heated effect he is having on you – not what you want to do to his thick hard salami! Unless, of course, you do have some plans for his, erm, sausage ...

Food fun: Put the fun back into your relationship courtesy of Mickey Rourke. Instead of supper, prepare a smorgasbord of edible delicacies. Then blindfold your man, and test his taste buds. Do people really do this? Give it a bash.

Touch down: Make time for a sensual massage ... for you, honey. Lay out the oil, a feather or some visual clues he will see. Light the candles (ultra flattering), turn on the heater, open a window near your intended position (nothing like erect nipples to let him think he's getting you hot) and let him know you will be waiting, naked after your shower, for him.

> *"We were in such post-baby bliss, that we made love in the hospital on the second day. But we used the lesser-used tunnel."*

LITTLE TART

Tired of playing mommy? Nothing will make you forget the baby monitor as fast as a little fantasy in a French chalet. Feel a bit silly? So what, do it anyway. Once the little darlings can open the door, fancy dress gets tough to explain. Now's your chance!

The schoolgirl. A short skirt, bobby socks, white shirt and tie askew. He's the teacher; you need help with your maths. You naughty thing.

The slut. Red lips, plunging neckline, no bra, short skirt. He is married and must resist. Make your move while he's in the study. Crawl under the desk and pucker up.

The dominatrix. Anything black, tight and preferably latex. Throw in a pair of kitchen gloves. The study's a good venue again. "Move off that chair and you will live to regret it …"

Doctor, doctor. Bring out the gloves again for this one. He's lying immobile, in a coma, you are a lush, randy nurse who will have her way. Props are everything.

French maid. Black and short with lacy apron. You are making up the room and bending from the waist. He is the lord of the manor and secretly watching you. You fight him off, but he's the boss.

The key to role-playing is to stay in character. It falls flat if you giggle or slip out of your role to make a comment. Accents make it far more fun.

> " I perfected the art of the blow job. I wanted to be intimate, but I did not want sex. "

ONE PERFECT BLOW

So you thought you had this one down? You may find that you're doing a whole lot more of it post-baby, so you might as well get it perfect. Some well-schooled gay friends helped us lay out exactly how to do your man right:

ACT ONE: THE WARM UP

Don't dive straight in – not unless you have the oral endurance of a professional athlete. Warm him up with some gentle stroking and a few tongue flicks over the entire penis and scrotum working up to the head. Make sure you cover the head thoroughly so it's slick and ready for your luscious lips.

ACT TWO: THE LONG RUN

When he's rearing to go, gently grasp the penis fairly low with one hand.

Your lips are covering your teeth at this point.

When its slick and wet start slipping your mouth down lower so it's dipping below the penis head each stroke (remember to gently draw the foreskin back if it's in the way). Create a slow but steady rhythm with your two hands and your mouth. Concentrate your mouth on the head, moving down to a couple of inches below its join and back up, and keep you hands moving in the same rhythm handling the shaft. You can slide your mouth lower down the shaft when you feel like it.

If you need to take a break keep your hands going and just move them up so they don't miss out the head and the inch below it. This is the most sensitive part of the penis and gives the most stimulation. If you want to call an end to the act seductively, ask what he wants next or move seamlessly on to hand stimulation with the occasional lick of the head.

ACT THREE: BLOWS FROM PROS

You can start adding a bit of variety to your technique, as long as you don't lose your beat. If your lips skip a step, just keep going with your hands.

Add some suction with your mouth for additional stimulation.

When you slide down the shaft, you can circle his head with your tongue or gently scrape along the penis with your teeth – if he screams it's too much tooth.

my story: Sirran

The first few months were no-go regarding sex. I simply was not interested. I was tired, emotional and my body felt everything except sexual. But I can honestly say that having a baby has improved my sex life immeasurably.

I always enjoyed sex. I was spontaneous and orgasmed with a little effort. I was fit, trim and healthy, but I was not deeply sensual. I feel like something was awakened within me after my birth. It was not immediate, but I felt a rising awareness of my body, its power, its incredible frailty and its remarkable ability. I could feel my pelvic muscles. They had been somehow triggered.

When my baby suckled, I could feel every sensation in my body. Then I developed a bladder problem and constantly felt my bladder was full. It was very strange, but the full bladder kept me in a constant state of arousal. I felt like a naughty little girl, getting stolen pleasure out of needing to wee. I did not act on my newfound lust yet – I think I was so engaged with the baby and coping with the new hours, that thought never moved into action. But months later, my husband started to notice my sudden interest. We restarted our sex life and our marriage moved into a gear I never imagined. Everything was intensified tenfold. Orgasms were earth-shattering events rather than warm waves. I trained myself to orgasm without clitoral stimulation for the first time and incorporated breathing techniques to enhance my orgasm.

I wouldn't say we were like eighteen-year-olds, bonking at every given chance. In fact, twice a week was probably the most frequent. But the quality of the sex was unsurpassed. Louis was delighted and scared at the same time. I was not voracious; I was just totally in touch with my sensuality. That was nine years ago and things have just improved every year. My friends often confide their boring sex lives and lack of desire. I know it's a place that's easy to be in. We were there before the baby, after seven years together. I could have let it slide. Louis could have too. But I guess we decided to explore our sexuality with each other, to work at keeping the spark going and to find our own pleasure.

Sure, there are months when we don't have sex. But it's rare.

We chose some years ago to invest in our sex life. It's the best investment we've made.

my story: Tamara

I walked out on my husband on our tenth wedding anniversary. I was thirty-eight and we had not had sex for six years.

I guess it was just after the birth of our second daughter that our sex life dwindled. It just never picked up. Six months before our anniversary, I realised we were fantastic friends, but the thought of having sex was faintly repulsive.

I knew I wanted more. I wanted a spark, an attraction. I packed my bags, took the kids and moved in with my sister. Shane was stunned, but not surprised. Neither of us was really.

Four months later, we sat down and decided to go for counselling – to see if there was anything to try and save. My instinct said no, but my vows made me say yes.

The therapist was optimistic. He said we had a great relationship, but we had just neglected to work on keeping a sexual one. He banned us from any contact except during his sessions.

I thought I knew Shane inside and out, but what was emerging was a stranger I knew nothing about. I found it exciting and scary at the same time, as he told me of his private visits to strip clubs, frequent masturbation and fantasies. I cried for all the years we had lost and how we had each buried our sexuality from the other. I raged and accused. He cried over my rejection of him, my tiredness, my unflinching focus on the girls, the way I would casually shrug him off. He punched a wall. I started dancing classes and yoga. I started to think about sex. It was like a little switch went on in me. My view of the world started to shift. I started to desire Shane. He was not sexless – it was me who had switched off. He had just stopped sharing his sexuality with me.

Eighteen months later I moved back home with the girls and we have been in a deeply satisfying relationship for four years now. We both work at keeping the spark alive. We schedule sex and we love it every time. Neither of us had forgotten how to ride the bicycle, we just could not find a way to get back on.

WORKING GIRL:
CARING AND CAREERING

"What's that on your car radio?" a colleague asked, as I yelled an order over "Row, Row, Row Your Boat". What he thought it was is puzzling, as it's difficult to mistake the voices of twelve 2-year-olds trilling out the words at the high end of their limited range. I am steering with my knees (women can do that) while mixing up a bottle of formula and taking the off-ramp at speed. The music can't go off or my child will scream and that's worse than any infant choir. I am sweating and it's midwinter.

"Look let's just confirm this all via email," I cut the conversation short. "Battery going. Mail me if you didn't get any of the details".

Multitasking is a woman's domain. But when you combine baby and work it is hilarious, that is, if you have time to laugh. It never crossed my mind that having a baby would change my work or ambition in any way. I would pop her out and be back to my old self four months later when my "leave" was over. I anticipated My Return with a frenzy usually only reserved for baked cheesecake or Prada slingbacks. In fact, so focused was I on my return, that I did not quite as appropriately plan my leave.

CHAPTER 10

WHEN IT CAME TO MOTHERHOOD, I SAW MADONNA AS MY ROLE MODEL. I ignored people who told me my life would change or that I might not want to spend every waking hour in my office or hovering over a skinny latte at the patisserie below.

I listened closely to people who said things like: "This baby must fit in with your life", or "Get out there quickly and get back to work. You will need to re-establish your life". Madonna did that. She was on set six months after having little Lourdes. There's something faintly sexy about having a dangerously busy life with multiple roles. It's a glamorous image really, one hand on the Graco stroller, baby bag slung over shoulder, laptop, crisp Malcolm Klûk suit with a low-cut top hinting at a woman who has a soft side.

You arrive home after a busy day, slip into a silk embroidered tunic and spend a lazy evening with the family, looking tired but radiant with love for the children and your blissful life.

It never crossed my mind that I would be raiding my "donate" pile for tie-dyed pants and a voluminous button up shirt for six months, nor that the waistband on my favourite pair of Klûk pants might never meet again. Nor that I would be dashing across town to a meeting in a pair of sweatpants with the "Wheels on the Bus" drowning out my daughter's screams from the back seat. Glamorous it was not.

"_I was sitting in a board meeting when I realised all I could think about was what Daniel was doing right now. Was he missing me? Was he crying? Who was comforting him? I had a physical pang that hit me in my heart chakra and just got worse and worse. When we broke for tea I called his nanny from the corridor and then found myself just weeping uncontrollably with love and blessings. It took all my self-control not to just rush home._ **"**

WORKING GIRL: CARING AND CAREERING

Neither glamorous nor much fun, which is why some months on I found myself spending less and less time at the office and more time at home.

There is a rising trend for millennium moms to stay at home and be done with nannies. Does this mean they are doing less than their Eighties counterparts? Quite the opposite. They are doing more. Stay at home does not mean lounging on the lawn with a cup of Earl Grey and wheat-free biscotti. Not only do we need to run a home-based business from our cellphones and G4 PowerBooks, we are downloading forty gigabytes of infant development information, stashing it on our iPods while packing in an evening course on baby massage and infant reflexology. We are steaming a batch of organic baby food with one hand and tapping out emails with the other while we sing "I'm a Little Teapot". And it's a song that demands performance.

We are in an age of technology-driven work. It's changed the world and the nature of work. We live on a new digital frontier. It's the new millennium and women are wired, hip and not threatened by men at work. Why would we be when men have handbags, wear concealer and have regular facials?

The more level playing fields do not mean women have become the new men. Fortunately shoulder pads and Melanie Griffith stayed in the Eighties. Hip new moms are relaxed, self-assured, big income earners. They know that a briefcase, boxy jacket and flesh-tone stockings mean dated, not serious.

"The sign on the gate of the playschool read 'Sorry moms – Jean is sick and we are closed today'. My world crashed. This could not be happening. I had to be in court in half an hour and I had nowhere to leave my kids."

Know your rights

Maternity leave has had a controversial history in South Africa, with endless rows between business and trade unions over how long it should be, whether it's paid, unpaid ... and who pays. It's an area wrought with anecdotes and stories of moms given luxurious six-month paid leave, to the gnashing teeth of moms told to clock back in at twelve weeks.

Expert legal eagle Keren Machanik says that these are your legal rights:

As it currently stands in South Africa, working women are entitled to four months unpaid maternity leave. This scenario is different all over the world. In Canada, those spoiled rotten moms get a year off for maternity leave and it's all paid up.

The four months kicks in a month before the baby is born and ends three months after the birth. If you would prefer to work to term and take the full four months after the birth, this can be altered if your doctor certifies you fit and well enough to do so. The additional month is a new benefit and was written into law by the Basic Conditions of Employment Act (BCEA) in 2002. Before that it was only three months unpaid leave.

High and dry

We've all got a friend who can kick back with six months paid leave, yet when you put your application in, you may be told that you are on your own to foot the bills. Why are so many women under the illusion that maternity leave is paid?

"Sometimes it is," Keren says. "There are some companies

that offer you a portion of, or even your full, salary. But this is discretionary and is by no means required by law. You can claim maternity benefits from UIF, but only if you work more than twenty-four hours a month for your employer and you are not remunerated on a commission basis. Many companies pay to make up the difference between your UIF benefits and your salary; some even pay up to 100 per cent. However, this depends on company policy and not on the law."

This means many women and families are hit with a double whammy: no salary and limited benefits from UIF.

If you are intending to claim from UIF, you must get your application to them eight weeks before childbirth or within six months after the birth to qualify. The UIF benefit payable to you is the difference between what your employer pays and the rate prescribed in the benefit schedule of the UIF Act and can never be more than 100 per cent of your normal salary. The schedule changes from time to time so it is advisable to check with the Department of Labour or with your company HR advisor about how it applies to your earnings.

If you do want to go back to work before your four months are up because you need the income or crave adult company, you should get a certificate stating that you are physically up to it from your doctor. The law clearly states that a woman may not work for six weeks after the birth of her child unless a medical practitioner or midwife certifies that she is fit to do so.

"The reason behind the law is protection of the employee and the unborn child," says Keren. "Not all women are desk-seated moms lounging behind a keyboard with a PA to bring them tea and there are, in fact, cases where being back at work could be hazardous to your or your child's health. Bear in mind that many women work in the clothing, textile and manufacturing industries. The objective of the law is really to prevent exploitation while you are pregnant and even after the birth of your child."

One stipulation is that no employer may require you to perform a job that is hazardous to your health or that of your child while you are pregnant or nursing. It further specifies that for a period of six months after the birth, the employer must actually offer you alternative suitable employment, on terms and conditions no less favourable than before you went on leave. This means that if you are on night shift or performing any job deemed hazardous, you can petition for another position until you stop nursing.

Keren says:

- Find out what the company policy is when you join it. Companies that do pay maternity leave sometimes require that you have worked for them for some time, often a year. If there is no company policy in place, the Basic Conditions of Employment will prevail.
- If you're a valued employee, a high-flier or bring in a lot of money for the company, you may have additional leverage to negotiate a strong maternity leave payment, and you can initiate discussions around terms.
- Let your company know that you are expecting a baby as soon as possible. You are not under obligation to tell them early, but it's good practice. You will also have far more room to negotiate your terms and conditions. Think about what you want before you sit down to discuss it with your manager.
- Anything is possible. You are entitled to negotiate flexitime or time-sharing if you don't want to return to work full time. There is nothing in the law preventing you from doing this

but also no obligation on your employer to agree to it. This will be a new condition of employment you are negotiating.

- The law states a full-time employee works forty hours a week – usually taken as eight-hour days. In some industries, these hours are less, and in some, they are more. How you work that out is your negotiation. A lunch break is not paid, so you can skip it and leave early. Or come in at 4am and leave by noon. Find a solution that suits your special circumstances and propose it. You never know, the company may just agree.

- You must notify your employer in writing at least a month before you intend to go on leave, stating the dates you want to start and end the leave. Keren advises that you notify them early on. "Do it when you feel comfortable, but as soon as possible. You don't want your manager finding out his prize creative is heading off on maternity leave from the office gossip."

- If you are seven months pregnant and haven't informed your employer in writing that you are indeed pregnant, you are breaching the conditions of your employment. You do have a duty to disclose your status. The later you leave it, the more difficult your negotiation.

TIME OUT

Annual leave. Paid. This is twenty-one consecutive days, but don't be fooled into thinking this is twenty-one working days. It is actually fifteen working days plus three weekends.

Sick leave. Paid. You are allowed thirty days within a three-year cycle. Sorry, this does not accumulate so if you don't take it annually, you lose it.

Maternity leave. Unpaid. Four months. If you miscarry in the third trimester or deliver stillborn you are entitled to six weeks maternity leave effective from delivery date.

Family responsibility leave. Paid. Three days a year for any justifiable event or family trauma for either gender. This is often taken as "paternity leave".

Unpaid leave. Ummm, unpaid. This one you discuss with your boss.

Remember these are the basic and minimum leave rights. However, in certain industries where a sectoral determination applies, these allocations may have been increased by negotiations between unions and employer.

Money does matter

Losing one income is a daunting prospect, no matter how much you are raking in. It's daunting because it means a whole new era of budgeting. But it's more daunting because it means that someone is going to have to support you. Not easy for a wild working girl.

Even if you have been married for many years, it's common that you have actually been running your finances separately. "You pay for that and I will cover this" is usually how it works. And what you have left over after a facial, full body massage, three pairs of kitten-heels and a splurge at the Mac counter at Edgars, you lob into the bond.

Stopping work has less to do with money than power. You have moved from an independent and successful earner to a dependent and clingy wife. It is a tough shift to make.

Cindy gave up her well-paid job in advertising to raise her son Cameron. "Tovay makes a good salary, and we did the sums and agreed he would support me. What we did not bank on was the feeling of powerlessness and dependency I felt. From an independent woman pulling a salary on par to his, I felt reduced to asking him for housekeeping money."

Meryl was an investment analyst and said losing her income almost cost her her marriage.

"I giggled with girlfriends about being a kept woman, but the reality was that I felt like one. Without my financial independence there was a shift in the balance of power that left me feeling insecure and petty. I felt I could not buy any luxuries and would attack him if he came home with CDs, clothes or anything I deemed an unnecessary expense. Mike made a packet. I just could not spend what I saw as 'his money'."

From a generous spender, Meryl became a penny-pincher who watched her family's finances like a miser. To help ease the stress financial issues put on your marriage, face up to the facts early.

"I saw myself as a boring homebody. My husband and I used to have stimulating debates about work, but all that ended. I convinced myself my opinion no longer mattered. I convinced myself he was having an affair with a sexy career girl while I was nursing our son in a washed-out old sundress."

How to drop the cleaver and talk money

- **Discuss your choices.** This is a financial decision as much as it is an emotional one. Separate the two issues. If you cannot afford it, you are going to have to reconcile yourself to going back to work.

- **Keep neutral.** Discussions about money are rarely well handled. Set a meeting time, keep to an agenda and make notes. Keeping the meeting on a professional footing will keep the issues clear. This is not a discussion to have in bed.
- **Weigh up your options.** Look at cutting your costs and discuss what you are prepared to sacrifice as a family. Work out the cost of childcare and nannies and weigh it against the loss of a salary. Remember that having a family does not mean you have to give up a career you love.
- **Remember you are a team.** You may want to give up work, but is it really feasible financially? While it was common for women of your mother's generation to become full-time moms, it is less common today. Look at your own perceptions; are you willing to consider a new way?
- **Set down timeframes.** Communicate whether you are stopping work for good or for four months. You can renegotiate, but you both need to have a long-term picture.
- **Get creative.** Close to sixty per cent of small businesses are run by women. Can you work from home? Can you create a flexi-time relationship with your employer?
- **Acknowledge your emotional space.** If you have never had family meetings about money before, get used to it as it's going to be a feature of life with kids. Clear the air. Let your partner know that you resist discussions on money, that you feel powerless, accused or defensive. Let him know that this is why you may react with anger, tears, denial or silence. Arm him with your manipulations and then sit down and have your meeting. At least when you attack with the cake knife he will know why.

Outta my way, I wanna work

What is it about the words "working mom" that can turn a jolly tea of tubby moms into a war zone. There is something about being a mother that wipes out years of humour and turns fun, vivacious girls into Serious Moms. Serious Moms put their child first. They are at every tea, every talk on child psychology. They bake gingerbread men and say things like: "Tilly is really making a mistake only giving Meg pulses, not complex proteins."

Serious Moms think other moms don't do things right. Being serious has nothing to do with whether you work or not. It has to do with the judgements you have against other moms. There are barbs on both sides of the fence. "Little Jenny is nine months and not even sitting," the full-time mom's conversation will go. "Yes, but don't forget that Judie works."

The working moms will snigger about toddler groups and ask what you do all day. If you think the most heated sites on the Internet are about politics and porn, think again. There are millions of moms online and they are fighting out a decades-old battle – to work or not to work?

Full-time moms are out to prove that there is no job tougher than raising kids. Sure thing, sister, with you on that one. They also say moms who work are neglecting their children in favour of their careers and find a litany of reasons why you need to spend twenty-four hours in your child's company (regardless of whether she is in playschool or not). Working moms either love their freedom or they are clogging up Internet chat rooms wanting advice on how to negotiate flexitime with their boss.

For sanity's sake, just make a choice and get on with it. You may want to scream at torch-carrying bloggers, but there's no need to wage a one-woman crusade. Do what makes you happy, and move on.

Ditch the guilt

- Be flexible. If you need a dual income and have to work, then acknowledge that that is your path right now.
- Acknowledge yourself. If you are the breadwinner, good for you. Instead of feeling resentful that you have to work, acknowledge your ability to earn good money. It's a talent. Stop wanting to be somewhere else.
- See your own need. Your child is actually fine. This child chose you because of who you are. It did not arrive expecting you to don an apron and give up your life for it. That would be horrific.
- Get rid of the guilt. What payoff are you getting from feeling guilty? Your perceived pressure to produce home-baked goods for the school cake sale or stimulate his fine motor skills with handmade beads come from you, not other moms and not your child. Do not fool yourself that it makes any difference to your child or anybody else whether you send a lopsided carrot cake or donate R20. It only makes a difference to you.
- Change it. The sheer energy wasted by the guilt, anger and gossip is not serving you. If you want to make a change, make it or get on with your life.
- Ignore the comments. You are going to get them and they are

"I agreed with my husband we would have two kids as it was his dream. It was never mine. Mine was senior vice-president by thirty-five. With each of the boys I took three weeks off work. We have two nannies and I spend the weekends with my boys without fail. If I travel they both come with their nannies. I was always there, but not hands on. Sometimes I think I have missed out on so much of their lives. But we have a great relationship and I know they love me."

never gonna stop. Do you really care what a complete stranger thinks of you? Where is your sense of self? Remember: if something someone says hits a nerve, then it has an element of truth for you. You may choose to use it or ignore it as you wish.

- Know that there is no right or wrong. How absurd to think there is a right way to raise a child or live your life. There are endless choices presented to you every moment on earth. Make peace with the ones you take and stop aiming for perfection. The most you can aim for is balance and self-knowledge.

Wired moms

The good news is, you can work and have children. The bad news is it's damn tough. Everything to do with babies is scheduled assuming you have the day at your disposal. Baby groups, clinic hours, swimming lessons are all excluded from the life of a working mom.

But that's assuming you are still holding on to an outdated notion of work.

Justine is a full-time mom. She also manages a restaurant franchise, designs board games and writes. In her spare time, she makes a solid income. Is she one extraordinarily talented gal? No, she simply uses technology and imagination. Lots of women do that.

Work can be fluid. Work does not have to mean a nine-to-five job. It is something you do that earns you money. That can mean going to an office and doing a job, but increasingly mothers are challenging that and changing the way they work. They don't do less. They just do things differently. They negotiate more suitable hours, they take work home or they use the technology on offer to be as productive as if they were in the office. They start their own companies; South Africa has a high rate of women entrepreneurs, which indicates that they are doing well and in increasing numbers.

Still, Keren cautions that SA companies are slow to agree to allow full time employees to work from home.

"It's tough for companies to police, regulate and manage. Companies have not yet found an effective way to monitor the associated costs. Like phone bills. How many calls are business, how many personal, how do you prove it? Is the stationery for your account or theirs? Also the facilities may be under query. Does the company now have to provide you with a fax machine, a PC, cellphone, photostat machine and courier service?"

"You do get companies who agree to a work-from-home setup, but it's still rare," she says. "They are more keen to have women taking on work from home during maternity leave, but with the knowledge that they will be coming back."

Eleven secrets for wired women

Get mobile: Cellphones, PDAs, laptops. Get moving. You can have a virtual office anywhere.

Lower your standards: Prioritise. You do not have to excel at everything. Pack the freezer with frozen meals, send your maid on a cooking course and stop picking up after everyone.

Caterers are king: Think those other moms actually cooked that lavish spread? What planet do you live on? Most delis, restaurants and catering firms will fill your dishes for a call and a small fee. Indian shops will do killer curries; just add some rice and sambals. Do you admit it? Absolutely, if asked.

Open accounts: Most pharmacies, groceries, video shops, dry cleaners and cafès will actually deliver to your house for a tiny fee, sometimes for free. This is a beautiful thing.

Internet shopping: Where would working moms be without online shopping at Pick 'n Pay and Woolworths? Having things delivered means you can skip the early evening rush to the shops and get straight home.

Do one thing at a time: Women are exceptional at multitasking. But the impact on your stress levels is huge. Stop trying to cram another thing in all the time. Concentrate your energy: your efficiency will rise and your anxiety reduce.

Perfection is boring: Do you really like those friends who are always on top of life? Chances are you have much more fun and more real relationships with friends who are just battling along with you. So why are you trying to be perfect? You will have far more fun if you are just yourself.

Don't ever lie: You will get caught and then it's a slippery slope. Let your work colleagues know that you have two kids and that your family comes first. Don't say you are going to a conference when you are heading to the moms' egg and spoon race at the nursery school. You will be seen.

Spread it out: What are grandparents, friends, godparents and neighbours for if not to be in your life and share the good stuff with you? Why do you feel you need to do it all yourself?

Have fun: It's not all work and kids. You also need to have fun, keep your sense of humour, nurture your marriage and exercise.

Act, don't think: If you want to restructure your time at work, do something about it. Don't bitch to co-workers and friends and turn the scenario over endlessly in your head – go straight to the right person and discuss it with them.

" I installed an office line in my study at home at my own cost and had my direct line for work diverted there. "

Get hired help

It never crossed my mind for a second not to have a nanny. In fact, so complete was my picture of domestic bliss with a trusting nanny with my baby securely strapped to her back, that I retrenched my gloriously efficient maid to hire a nanny who looked more the part. Our long-term cleaner Beauty did not fit my picture of a nanny with her single-syllable English, rake-thin build and boundless energy. I wanted someone who looked like, well, a nanny. We hired Nancy through an agency. She had lots of certificates, a back as broad as it was high, winked when she spoke and giggled a lot. I was in nanny heaven. She would be more than a nanny; she would be a friend and mother.

It was on her first day at work that I discovered she had recently had a stroke that left her mental faculties impaired. She found it difficult to compute the mechanism on the blinds and walking up the stairs was a morning's challenge. The idea that I would leave my newborn child with her was faintly ludicrous. We negotiated a rapid and guilt-steeped retrenchment and breathed a sigh of relief.

I was on the phone to Beauty immediately. I was under no illusion that I was going to do it all myself. Apparently everyone else was. Try rocking up at a mom's breakfast without baby in tow. A big mistake: the girls have all got their tots in hand and expect to see you with the baby.

You learn fast, sister. I would rush from the office to fetch Ruby to meet the girls for lunch then dash her back home.

Kirsten is an actress and producer and decided she was going to stay at home for two years with her firstborn and do it all herself.

"I totally immersed myself in being a mom. Chloe did not leave my side for nine months and I loved it. I slept in a camp bed in her room and only started solids when she was eight months. I wanted to do it all 100 per cent. I made homemade organic yoghurt, massaged her daily and continually stimulated her development. I think all the attention really paid off as she is far more developed that the other kids in our playgroup."

Fun while it lasted, but Kirsten was offered a fantastic job and accepted it on the spur of the moment. "I hired a nanny and spent two weeks training her before the job started.

"The first day at work was like a new beginning for me. I felt reinvented, powerful and free. I felt as if I had stepped out of a parallel universe and back into a life I knew. I almost wept with relief."

Will Kirsten stay at home with her second child? "Sure, for four months tops."

INVEST IN THE RELATIONSHIP

This is a long-term relationship and you need to treat it with the respect it deserves. To pay below a suitable rate is like driving with worn brakes. You do not want a bargain nanny, you want a good nanny.

Look for someone you feel can grow with your child.

You will need to invest your own time in making sure they know your house, your family and your needs, and you may want to invest some money in sending them on childcare, safety or cooking courses that will put your mind at ease, and empower them to feel confident with your baby.

"My mother keeps telling me I will regret this time I am not spending with my child. It irks me, but I know that I have more than enough to give everyone, as well as myself."

PUT IT IN WRITING

This does not only apply to your employment contract but also to your expectations and household duties.

Write a detailed list of your baby's schedule, feeding habits, menus and emergency contact numbers and details and paste it up in the kitchen.

Go over it regularly with the nanny, and note any changes.

This list will continually be updated as your baby grows and its needs and schedule changes. Put it in writing. Your clarity will give your nanny peace of mind.

FIND THE RIGHT NANNY FOR YOU

You think looking for a good man is tough? Try finding a nanny you are going to trust with your precious baby. Whether they live in, work part-time or just come in for the odd day, this person is going to become a central figure in your house and will require your implicit trust. Like any good long-term relationship, don't be dazzled by good looks and rather look for more reliable and enduring qualities.

FIRST BASE

The first interview is your chance to get a good feel for the person and to see if they have the personality traits as well as qualifications for the job. Don't rush the process. Interview a few candidates so you can compare personalities and your response to them.

UP CLOSE AND PERSONAL

Feel free to ask about their background. This person will become part of your family and you need to know this stuff. Ask open-ended questions that will draw them out and do not be afraid to cover the same territory again if you feel it was not answered properly.

- Tell me about the children on your last job.
- Tell me about your family background and childhood.
- Do you have children, how many, and where do they live?
- What are your goals?
- Do you have a partner, what does he do, does he live with you?
- What do you enjoy doing in your spare time?

TIP:

Looking after a baby and cleaning a house is physically demanding stuff. Are they up for it?

THE PROFESSIONAL

Whether you go through an agency, a classified ad or a friend's recommendation, you need to make sure they have the professional experience for the job you require.

ASK QUESTIONS LIKE:

- Tell me about your relationship with your last two employers and what you did for them.
- What ages of children have you worked with?
- If asked for a reference, what would your last employer say about you?
- Have you ever been confronted with an emergency situation at work?
- What happened and how did you respond?

TIPS:

- Go over any courses or childcare related training they may have done and ask to see certificates.
- Get as many references as you can, and thoroughly check them.

SECOND BASE

You have now gone through a few interviews and want to see more of the candidate and possibly organise them starting on a part-time trial basis. The foreplay is over and it's now time to get into the real detail of each task, baby duties and routine, household duties, hours, salary, benefits and expectations. Discuss each task in detail, and type up a detailed list that outlines each task and when it is scheduled (daily, weekly, monthly).

There are firm and fair laws that govern domestic work. It is worth your while spending ten minutes reading the easy guides on the Department of Labour's website before you type up a contract detailing the nitty gritty like working hours, overtime and leave (www.labour.gov.za and follow the interest group links to "domestic workers").

my story: Kgomotoso

I wanted to be more than my mother. She had given up her life for her kids and I held it against her. I held her cloying love, her lack of sense of self and her devotion to her children against her. When we all left home she floundered like a small child without an aim in life. Ten years on, she has not found that focus. She had no avenue to pursue other than us. It scared me to death and drove me to graduate the youngest and brightest in my accounting class.

I was never going to be a mother. I always wanted children, but I was going to be more than a mom. I was going to be important, respected. Famous even, if truth be told. My first son crept up on me, and I was back at work after three months. I was promoted to partner a year later. Then my second son arrived. My return to work was celebrated. I was taking strain, but my work was me. I bulleted out of the house with a sense of relief every morning. Work stress was familiar ground for me. We had a fantastic income and a full-time nanny. And, of course, there was my mom.

Then I fell pregnant for a third time. You would think I missed the bit on how to use protection, but all three times were despite all precautions. My third pregnancy hit me like a ton of bricks. We needed two maids to cope with the joint hours. I was exhausted. The years of flat-out mania came crashing down. I started sneaking in sleeps during work. Then I resigned. I was the shining star; tipped for senior partner the next year and I had just hit a crunch. Take some time. You'll come back, they said. I smiled reassuringly.

Staying at home brought up all my fears. I was dependent on my husband, lonely and sad. I was becoming my mom. There were times I loved it, loved the hours of fun with my three. But I wanted more. I wanted more travel, more stimulating debates. I wanted myself back. My kids gave me unimaginable joy, but they could not fulfill me like I could fulfill myself. I went back to work when my youngest was four. It was a long time at home. It became easier, but I was not a natural at it. It's different now. It's more balanced. I feel more powerful. I know better. Now, I say no. I go home at five and I don't work weekends. I am just as good. In fact, I am better.

HANG TOUGH:

CAN YOUR RELATIONSHIPS SURVIVE YOUR BABY?

On good evenings, Belle used to dance on tables in between the empty tequila bottles and ashtrays. She and Ryan, her partner of three years, met on the dance floor and cemented the attraction over a line of coke on the toilet seat. They were both lawyers and their group of friends was wide and wild. They hooked up on a Friday night and the party only ended on Sunday afternoon.

Then she fell pregnant. "Just nine months and I will be back on the circuit," she told her friends. She squeezed her ballooning tummy into increasingly sexier Lycra dresses, danced the night away in stilettos and billed ten-hour days.

The whole way through her pregnancy she maintained her only craving was for tequila. "Hold the lemon, I'll do it straight-up the second he comes out," she would cry as she passed on another round of drinks, in a late night club. She rode her pregnancy like a cowgirl on a bronco. Sexy, sassy and stylish, she was the epitome of fun. Nine months of clean living and she could not wait to get back on the party circuit.

CHAPTER 11

THEN SETH UNEXPECTEDLY ARRIVED ON A COLD WINTER'S MORNING. He was eight weeks early and had breathing complications. Belle spent eighteen hours a day at the hospital, either expressing milk or feeding Seth. Friends came with presents and champagne. Belle thanked them but declined the bubbly. Ryan toasted every visitor. The trickle dwindled and still Belle stayed. After three weeks, she brought Seth home, kangarooed him in her shirt and kept him close. Ryan was out every night with the gang. Sometimes they all came over and had drinks before hitting the town. Belle was polite but excused herself to breastfeed. Eyebrows were raised. Ryan was toasted for tolerating her moodiness.

"I realised that Ryan and I had had three years of parties and fun. Now life was not fun, we had no common ground. In the cold light of day – sober, straight and suddenly a mom – I realised that I did not even like the man, least of all want to share a life and a child with him. We had nothing to say to each other. He loves his son and I know that he will be a loving father, but without the parties, we had no relationship."

Belle's isolation extended to her friends. "They were a good-time gang, and I was not having a good time. We had shared crazy nights, clubs, trips and hard work. But we had shared nothing real, nothing of the heart and soul. I realised that when I needed support and friendship with Seth's struggle, true friends are more valuable than gold. And that I had none."

Her story is not unique. Childbirth is a life-changing event. It means your entire life can and often does change irrevocably. Call it a re-purposing or a re-positioning of your destiny. Priorities shift, meaningless stuff suddenly has meaning and things you held precious, fall away. Sometimes it means losing old friends. Sometimes, as in Belle's case, it means losing a partner.

Your man

Being a parent is revoltingly romanticised. Nobody told you having a baby was going to put serious strain on your relationship. Most of the advice we are given before we have children is about giving up sleep, or smug smiles and "wait and see" jibes. Nobody tells you that an explosion is about to happen in your relationship and that the two of you are going to have to work really hard to survive it intact. If truth be told, if many couples knew what becoming parents was really about, there would be far fewer children in the world today.

Let's get this out of the way straight off: Having a baby does your relationship no favours. It is certainly no way to mend a relationship. It may even be truer to say that, if your relationship is not open, honest and functioning, having a child creates a strong chance of destroying it. You've got a lot of work to do to keep it on track. That is, if you are still married after the hormonal thunderstorm that possessed your body during pregnancy. Well, hang in there, the rocky ride is not over yet. A power-play will emerge over the first few months of your baby's life, that will see you fighting like ... well, like your parents used to.

And let's say it again now – your relationship will never be the same again. Never.

" It was like some sort of switch went on in the last few weeks of the pregnancy. I started nesting, and a year later I haven't stopped. Out came the old family recipe books and the old Pfaff sewing machine. Before I could say 'crochet' I was basting roast chickens and planting rosemary in the garden. Oh God, I thought, I am living in Martha's Vineyard. But I just went with the whole process. My husband loved it, which irked me no end. But I wasn't going to let his reaction spoil my fun. "

Things will settle down and you will find a new equilibrium, but your old relationship is gone forever and your task, as partners, is now to define a new one. Sounds exciting, gulp.

Take heart in that this is a necessary readjustment and it will probably emerge better, but there is no going back now. Your relationship has moved from that of lovers to parents.

What has changed?

Time: You are lying cuddling on a Sunday morning. The sun has not yet risen, but you have been up all night. He looks over at you tenderly. Your heart melts despite the night of rowing over who will pacify the tiny terrorist, bellowing for a bottle next door.

"Sweetheart," he says.

"Yes," you flirt back. Your pulse starting to race like it hasn't in years.

"Let's bring Connor through to cuddle."

The spare time you had used to be spent with each other. Now you have two problems: You have almost no spare time and there is a third person who needs to share any downtime you do have.

" I am having a career girl backlash. I have worked since the day I left school, consistently and successfully. Then I took two months maternity leave, and I realised what I have been missing out on. My husband had been pressuring me to take full-time leave, to bring up our son and I took him up on it. It was incredibly scary. We had never discussed our finances. We never had to as we both earned very good salaries. We are still finding a good way to communicate around money – an emotional subject for me now. But the licence not to work has been an incredible joy in my life. I am sure I will go back eventually, but for now, I am relishing being a full-time mom. "

You: You are both transformed people. You are parents.

Your family: Now you have one. You have a new person in the house who is not going to pass unnoticed. You have created an entire new being with its own personality, who is going to start to exert himself. This creates an additional dynamic in the family that will see a realignment of your relationship to accommodate this new life.

Money: Babies are expensive. If the initial setup with pram, car seat, nappies, clothes, bottles, dummies and squeaky toys you never get to use has not sunk you, the monthly maintenance costs of your small addition will add up and slowly erode what used to be a sizeable disposable income. Add the loss of your income to the pot and your relationship dynamic has changed. No more Mr Delivery and Woolworths organic section, you are now lugging home bulk packs of instant noodles from Makro. Fortunately, you have less to spend your money on now that dinners out and glorious weekends out of town are hazy memories anyway.

Even if you have more than enough to go around, the fact that you are not working leads to a power shift that is tough to get used to. Arguments over money are a certain in every relationship.

Gender bender: Last month you were too busy launching a campaign to even call to cancel dinner. Now you have left seven "What time are you coming home?" messages and it's only 11am. God help him when he comes through the door. You are on to him like a tornado – flinging accusations and guilt. You will not stop, until he feels as bad as you do. Until he knows what a tough day you've had, just how lonely you are, and how little time you have had to yourself.

The only pants you will be wearing during this time are waist-

> **"** *I am finding being supported by my husband a massive strain. It is making me insecure, petty and guilty. He is relaxed about it; it's me who can't cope.* **"**

high nylons, a very distant cousin of sexy French full-cut knickers. Forget about being the boss: this is not the time in your life when you will be the one steering the ship.

Your hip-and-happening relationship has just hit a time warp back into the Fifties. You are at home with a baby on the hip and your man is out working to support you. You are a walking cliché. Ouch, it's gotta hurt.

The gender patterning that emerges in a new family is centuries old. It is primordial and it is largely inescapable. The care for the baby rests with you. You will take total responsibility for her – her food, entertainment, wellbeing and logistics. Your husband has become the breadwinner.

This is a big thing for a career girl who is used to being an equal earning partner in the relationship. This is a tough one. From having your accountant and lawyer on speed-dial, you are swept into a power shift that is unfathomable to a hip and urbane girl. You are becoming your own worst nightmare. If this were *Fear Factor*, they'd have discovered your weakness: being a needy, dependent and emotional woman. And you are now one of them.

Worse. You are your mother.

Babies don't have to ruin your marriage

YOUR RELATIONSHIP IS YOUR FIRST PRIORITY

During the first year, there is an overwhelming protective instinct and you know that your baby comes first. This is a damaging blow to a relationship. It means you are putting your child before each other. This will change and needs to change but it may take longer than a year to start taking effect. There will come a time when you need to realise that you and your partner must come

" I realised how few real friends I had. The types I could call at 2pm on a Saturday and say: 'Please help, I am desperate. Will you take my baby for an hour?' It forced me to re-evaluate my life and realise that I urgently needed some strong girlfriends. It's just that making them is not that easy. "

first. Your relationship was there before the baby arrived and it will be there long after he has left. You need to protect it. Your child is a product of your relationship; he or she cannot replace it.

A CHILD CANNOT DESTROY YOUR RELATIONSHIP

Only you can do that. Children are simply out there, in the world, being themselves. They are needy, demanding and want to be perfectly loved. They will fill your house for a few years, and then they will move on and have their own families. They have no role in your relationship and can neither strengthen nor destroy it. It is your inability to renegotiate you relationship that can destroy it.

YOU ARE RESPONSIBLE FOR YOUR OWN HAPPINESS

Nobody can ever fulfill you but yourself. Not your life partner, not your child, not your friends. A marriage is a place in which you have the space to go on your own journey. Work to understand more of yourself, to become more of yourself.

THERE IS NO SUCH THING AS FOREVER

Being in a relationship is a choice you make every day. Sometimes you don't know why you have made that choice. You are there because you have chosen it and it is part of your journey. If you do want to end a relationship, be sure that overcoming this hurdle is not part of your journey, in this relationship. Nobody is perfect – that would just be boring.

Seven deadly relationship myths

1. I can change him

Get that out of your head. You can never change anybody but yourself. The most you can hope to do is grow enough yourself to find acceptance and to understand why you think you know better than he does.

2. We need to have the same interests

What for? One of the biggest mistakes couples make is to think they need to acquire each other's interests, travel together, work or play together. You are different people. You have different pasts, genders and agendas. You will not make your relationship any stronger by becoming more alike. You may well make it stronger by becoming more of yourself. Get your own life.

3. There is an "us"

There is no such thing. There is you and him. Don't make the mistake of assuming you are going to think as a unit about money, sex, discipline, movies – the list is eternal. You are both individuals, each on your own paths through life. You are walking next to each other right now; you have a child together, but NEVER think you are one.

4. I understand how he thinks

If you even understand how you think, you are up there with the Dalai Llama, let alone understanding how any other person on this earth thinks. The best you can do is hear his reasons.

5. Fighting means we are not compatible

A strong relationship has conflict at its core. Everybody fights –

just watch your kids. Being an adult just means you get a whole lot better at it.

What you need to get better at, is finding a way of disagreeing that does not need to destroy you, frighten the kids or get your blood pressure into the danger zone.

6. Sex is not important

Sex shifts your relationship from that of friends to an intimacy, sharing and closeness that is unique with only one person. With all the new things you share as a couple, it's easy to let sex slide out of the picture. It's also easy to get fat and unhealthy, but your life together will be more enriched if you can choose the less easy route and work on your sex life.

7. Love is forever

Never ever assume this is forever, least of all that your love may be consistent over a lifetime together. Love only happens in the moment. If truth be told, you probably love each other ten per cent of the time, hate each other ten per cent and eighty per cent of the time, you are indifferent.

There is no sitting on your laurels in life, especially not in your relationship. You both change every day, you grow in different ways and for two people to walk next to each other along this rocky path, you need to work your relationship constantly, or you are going to wake up one day without one.

" Weekends loom like a migraine. My husband usually works most of the weekend and after a long week's work, I know it will be nothing for me, but more hard work all weekend looking after my son. I wish I had girlfriends to share the load with. "

SPACE SAVERS

DON'T JUST SHARE THE BAD STUFF:

Geena says: "I copied my husband on an email I sent my girlfriends on the joys of motherhood and he was very taken aback. He said that all I ever share with him is my frustration, anger, resentment and loss of my life. He had no idea that I was enjoying even a day of it. I realised that I find it easy to share the bad stuff, but not so easy to share the goodies."

DON'T MAKE YOUR MOOD HIS PROBLEM:

There are days when you just want to rage. There is no problem with that, as long as you don't take it out on your husband or think that your mood has anything to do with him.

Just explain that you are frustrated, have cabin fever and are in an incredible mood – but it's got nothing to do with him and he cannot make you feel better. Better still, take yourself off somewhere and have a good scream, then come back into the relationship clear.

FIND A CLAWING POST OTHER THAN YOUR HUSBAND:

Buy a punching bag, go for a long hard run, lock the door, run a warm bath and cry your heart out. Get all that sadness and anger out, just don't take it out on your relationship.

LEAVE THE PAST BEHIND YOU:

The first year is a rough ride. It is not always going to be this way and your relationship will find a new level, but don't try and move back into the past, when it was just the two of you. Just stay in the moment, acknowledge the reality of your life and find new ways of relating to each other.

Relationship savers

SET SOME RULES

Every relationship has rules. But relationships are dynamic and the rules will change or you will want new ones. You both need to sit down and agree on the rules. Set different ground rules for the family. These are just for you.

1. Limit kiddie conversation: At some point, you need a ground rule about how much conversation the two of you have that revolves around your child. Your relationship was diverse and exciting. There is more to your relationship than your offspring.

2. Keep date night: Just the two of you and keep it no matter what. At no time during the date are you allowed to mention your child (well, try it).

3. Get physical: Restart your sex life.

4. Communicate: Communication is really the best you can do in any relationship. No matter what you are going through, share it with the other person.

" I am so needy for my husband. I resent his time alone and the relative normality of his life. "

Girlfriends

It is very easy during the first year of having a baby, to find yourself in a very lonely place. This is worse if you stop work. Your life now revolves around a small baby and you are spending most of your time alone. Sure, friends call and stop in, but they have to leave again. Even busy career girls feel the crushing isolation and loneliness that comes with having to put your baby first.

Having family around lessens the blow, but you are still the one holding the reins, long after everyone goes home. If you do not have family you can rely on, the first year can be one of the most achingly lonely times of your life.

How do I make friends?

Join a club: Thought this advice was only dished out to desperate wallflowers with wire braces and library memberships? Think again. Fortunately, there are lots of groups that cater for cultural snobs like you. If the idea of singing "Humpty Dumpty" along with twenty other boisterous moms brings on a panic attack, try yoga, play-groups, post-natal tea groups, swimming classes for babes, baby massage classes. You need to be proactive. You will be surprised what fab girls you will meet. Why, they are just like you!

" I have no family around, and I feel like I am really alone in rearing my child. I long for a granny to just step in and take my daughter for a day. "

Networking: Women en masse scare me silly. I have a picture of organised girl get-togethers that is a nightmarish scene from *Steel Magnolias*, but we are all wearing shower caps. My first bout of pregnancy nausea came during antenatal classes when a fellow scholar excitedly shared how she and her friends babysat each other's children and breastfeeding was included on the menu. Call me an ice

> **"** I woke up one day and said: 'I am going to make myself some friends.' I realised I could either keep on moping for months or do something about it. I felt like a twelve-year-old going to a new school. Two months later, I had met the most fantastic group of girls through a baby massage course, and we meet once a week for tea. **"**

queen, but I am not ready for the nipple kibbutz quite yet.

I am a reformed girlfriend. I cannot get enough women in my life right now because I have learned, the hard way, that if there is one resource you cannot live without with children, it is a network of friends with babies.

It is absolutely critical to start building a support network of friends and family for yourself. This is going to become more and more critical as your child grows. So start now.

Ask for help: Friends do actually want to help out and be a part of your child's life. It's your turn to trust them and include them in your new life. Pick up the phone to a friend with a baby of a similar age and make a date. Make yourself supportable.

Be supportive: Offer support back. You know what it's like, so make a plan with a friend along the lines of: "You take Brian on Saturday afternoons and I will look after Rupert on Wednesday mornings, so you can go back to yoga." This is new territory for you. You have been so busy crawling around in self-pity, you may have forgotten you can also lend a hand to someone else.

Initiate contact: Realise that other moms out there could be feeling the same way you do. If you bump into someone and strike up a good conversation, invite them somewhere: "I am having a whole group of new moms for tea and a chat on Monday.

> **"** I took being a mom far too seriously for about two years. I was a real pain. An awful row with a friend suddenly turned the light on. I was so busy being a mommy, I had left myself somewhere behind. **"**

"I am becoming my mother. God help me."

They would all love to meet you. Let me email you the details", or "A whole group of us are going to start baby swimming lessons. Why don't you join?" You could have a fantastic new friend there.

Make peace with yourself: You have a gorgeous baby to spend lots of time with. Stop wishing you were somewhere else. In a few years she or he will be off to school and have no time for you and you will be hankering after these lonely days alone with her or him. Your social life will return, preschool and school will present you with a social life you would pay to outsource. Enjoy this lonely time.

"It's hard work to play two roles: mother and lover. But I find if I put in the effort, it pays off endlessly in our relationship."

Can your friends survive your baby?

Moving from manicures and weekly massages to clinic weigh-ins and red eyes is a radical lifestyle change. The question is, can your old friends survive your baby?

The answer is yes. But you are going to lose one or two along the way.

Most often, the friends you will lose are those without babies. Why?

- You've changed. Your life is no longer spontaneous, carefree and fun.

"I can't relate to my oldest friend since she had her baby. She has this unbearably smug tone that makes me feel I just have no idea about life at all and she does."

- You are no longer Miss Congeniality. Getting out of the house takes forty-five minutes and driving there you will already start to wonder if it was worth it.

- You're bored with drinking. All night parties are non-negotiable and weaving down the corridor to settle your baby with a stomach full of Cosmopolitans is not an option.

- Hangovers are no longer permitted. Not when there is a bright-eyed little beauty wanting all your attention all day.

You're a regular dream guest. All you can talk about is your shrinking uterus, nipple creams and the texture of pooh (thankfully, not yours). Little wonder your friends check their watches five times during tea with you. You're downright boring.

Even with a baby, there is a limit to which you can engage in baby talk with others. Some moms, however, don't have this intolerance. Somehow, they think that the minutiae of their lives will make fascinating dinner party fodder. But watch everybody roll their eyes, if not leave the room, as one approaches at a party. We call them Glowing Moms. Everything is exciting to them and they feel that it should equally titillate everyone else. Lack of sleep or full night's sleep, formula or breast, pooh, wee, nappies, bum rashes, vomits, teeth.

Yawn. Will someone shut her up?

But it's you. And you're doing it again and again. It's uncontrollable. The truth is, this is your life right now – it's an endless circle of bodily fluids and burps. Just remember, it will change. You will start to re-establish old patterns and interests and you will probably want your friends back.

Get invited twice:

- Restrict the baby talk to friends with common interests. Grandparents are an exception. Here nothing is too long-winded or boring.

" I can barely remember what I used to talk about. At one point in a conversation with an old friend I said: 'Enough baby talk, let's talk about something else.' There was a long silence. So long it was unbearable. I felt like I was stuck at a dinner table, eyeballing a blind date. Maybe it was too much pressure, or maybe we have nothing in common right now. "

- Never use baby-speak with friends. Talking about botties, doo-doo and blankies has no place in an adult conversation.
- Diversify. You used to have other interests. Remember those days? If you don't remember, at least pretend you do. Baby groups and swimming lessons don't count.
- Confess. Tell your friends you have a terminal fear that you are boring them to death. They will lie and tell you it's all fascinating to them because they love you that much. Ask them to let you know if you meander on to baby talk again during your monthly lunch with the single gals.
- Put away that photo album of your birth. It's strictly for family functions and medical seminars now.
- Let yourself off the hook. This is where your life is right now. Of course you are going to talk about it, like when you are eighty you will talk about the importance of fibre and the rising cost of retirement complexes. It's boring, but it's you.

In-laws and grandparents

Few things can sour your mood as quickly as a visit from in-laws.

No matter how well you connect with your in-laws, there are going to be moments when you want them dead.

This is new terrain for all of you. You have borne their grandchild and, love you as they may, they are going to love him more. His wellbeing is their utmost concern and there are times when

" I adore Peter's mom, but the second she touches Kaitlin, I see red. For no reason my mood blackens and I get bossy, critical and interfering. It brings out the worst in me to the point where I undermine everything she says. She is so happy just to have spent time with Kaitlin that she ignores it. After the visit, I want to kick myself. "

they think you are not doing the right thing. The first few months are going to be the toughest. They have had children, you are new to the game, and everything you do is going to be "corrected".

It is important to remember that they can be both right and wrong. First, they have a wealth of personal experience and that rates higher than book knowledge or ideas. They are sharing what worked for them in the hope that it will work for you too. There is a strong chance that some of the tips or methods they offer you may be valuable and it is certainly worth considering. Second, their knowledge comes from at least twenty years ago. A lot has changed since your husband was a baby, certainly science has moved fast and many new facts have emerged. The best bet is to measure up their methods against knowledge you have gained and then choose the course of action you are most comfortable with.

But the most important thing to realise is that your in-laws are your greatest babysitters. They love your baby, they (mostly) know what they're doing and they're free!

> *"I would call my mom at two o'clock in the morning to ask her questions about burping or fevers. She would always be there, and never mention the time."*

Mamma me

Regardless of the twists and turns your relationship with your mother has taken over the past few decades, you are going to want to clone her in the months after your baby arrives. For many women, their transition to motherhood is the start of a new, improved relationship with their mothers. Friends come and visit and then go, but your mother is the bedrock of your first few months. Whether she is there from the birth, mucking in to run your house and bring you chicken soup in bed, or swoops in weeks later to take control of the situation, you will allow yourself to become a pitiful and teary-eyed wreck in the presence of

> *"I spent thousands in phone bills to my mother from the UK. She stayed with me for three weeks, but when she went back, I would call her for advice on every little thing."*

> *"The second my mother-in-law steps through the door my chest starts constricting. She talks to me in this baby voice, referring to me as 'mom' as if she is actually having the conversation with my son about me."*

this woman. She can see you at your very lowest ebb and still tell you how glorious you look.

Don't, however, assume that she will be as trusted in looking after your baby as she is in soothing you. This is not necessarily the case and you may find you do not want to leave your baby in her paws for more than a few minutes. That is, until you relax enough and then you will be belting over to her house to dump the load at every opportunity. The intensity of the bond you develop with your mother over these months is not diminished by distance, and women find themselves relying on their moms, living across oceans, more than on a friend around the block. Does this momma-bliss honeymoon end? Of course, she will drive you nutty within a few months with her tendency to ride the clutch or the way she cling-wraps your cheese every time she visits. But the cycle of your relationship has changed and a new bond has been created. You have a glimpse of the unconditional love she gave to you. And you know for sure she once handled your privates as closely as you alone have.

Train the old folks

Keep your sanity, without it all ending in tears.

> *"The second he had a dirty nappy, she would hand him straight back to me saying: 'There we go mom, we need a change.' Grrrrrr.*

Just say yes. It doesn't harm you. It will make them feel like they have given you advice of value and it makes the world a nicer place. Say yes, and then do it your way. Remember that they had their own children thirty years ago, and they have forgotten a lot.

Stand your ground. There is no need to have a row, but you need to make it clear that you rule the roost. If you don't want your child to eat meat, they are going to have to respect that.

" My mother-in-law is pushing me to put rice porridge in my son's night-time bottle. She says she did that to Mike when he was six weeks and is so insistent that I have to bite my tongue. All the books say it may damage the digestive system. "

Communicate clearly. Don't assume they know your preferences and then get angry when they do things a different way.

Handle things with the correct person. Go to the source. Don't have a bitch session to your husband about something his mother has done. It's got nothing to do with him. Call her up and calmly just tell her that you would have preferred her to handle it a different way.

Back off. Grandparents will forge their own relationships with your child, so let them do it their way. You cannot stand in the way of that. You are not the only person who loves your child. Thank heavens for that.

Be specific. Hand a detailed list to the grandparents along with your child. If you are following a strict routine, they must know what it is and follow it to the letter. It will clear things up for them, give you peace of mind and make the day easier for both of you. List the meal or bottle times, snack times, juice times, bath time, bedtime. Be specific about what she gets at each meal.

Know they come from love. Stop thinking this is about you. They are doing what they think is the very best for their grandchild, not what they think is going to annoy you. Give them the space to give their best to him, even if it doesn't suit you.

" There was my 72-year-old father-in-law, bending over his grandson, playing peekaboo, with the energy and range of motion an eighteen-year-old would struggle to imitate. I had to laugh. "

my story: Louise

I was eight weeks into my baby fog when I got a call from an old friend. So old in fact, that I could barely place him. He reminded me that we had worked together on a two-week corporate video shoot covering a corporate golf challenge in 1988. I vaguely recalled that we had gone for coffee a few times over the fifteen-year gap, mostly touching base on work contacts.

He had heard I had a baby, he was in town and would love to come and see my baby.

Flattered that I had meant so much to him, I agreed. "Pop over for a quick tea tomorrow morning," I offered, still battling to remember the man.

When he arrived, I remembered his nickname used to be Prawn due to an uncanny red hue to his skin. There was much speculation as to whether this was caused by his penchant for brandy and Coke or years of exposure to the sun. Turns out it was genetic.

The morning got off to a bad start. Sebastian had just gone to sleep so conversation points were limited, but long silences did not seem to bother him. The visit stretched from three pots of tea into mid afternoon. Tactful hints for the Prawn to leave had made way to bald statements of request.

"I am going to breastfeed Sebastian," I said with a theatrical overemphasis on breast. "I will be quite some time so Magdaline will let you out. Lovely seeing you."

I strolled back downstairs, thirty minutes later, slipping a disposable breast pad into my bra. There he was, immersed in Tony's *National Geographic* collection.

"Why are you still here?" I found the tone that had won me SRC rep in '91.

"I hope I am not inconvenient," the Prawn said looking sheepish. "I am only in town for a day and without transport. I was going to ask for a lift, but I can see you don't want to leave the house. A friend will collect me but can only get here after 3pm."

The house is large and roomy. He could pass unnoticed for a few hours and he was clearly a sad, lonely man. But an emotional mother with leaking breasts and pink J-Lo velour tracksuit pants is not strong on sympathy.

Not fifteen minutes later, the taxi I had summoned arrived to dump him at the nearby shopping mall. I paid for the ride with a wide smile, but there was no hiding that this was not a humanitarian gesture between friends.

It was a case of "leave or I will have you arrested".

my story: Keara-Lee

I lost my oldest and dearest friend when I gave birth. Tracy and I had met, aged eight, when I broke her nose falling off the slide. We had never looked back and had grown up together. She had been my bridesmaid and I hers. We spent most days together and were really more family than friends. During the last month of my pregnancy, I went through an emotional roller-coaster that I had never experienced in my life before. I cried non-stop.

I isolated myself totally and stopped going out. I went to work, came home, bathed, watched TV and went to bed. My life was singular and I loved it. Nobody else mattered but me, my warm house and my husband.

Then Tessa arrived and I was thrown into six weeks of just trying to cope. I had birth complications and my focus was on myself and my own healing. I cut myself off from everyone. My husband fielded all my calls, visitors were turned away and my mom flew down from Zimbabwe to help out. I emerged, after six weeks, feeling almost ready to face the world. I finally felt I could pick up the phone without weeping or see friends, without terror at how my life had changed or how I was going to cope.

I was in for a shock. My friends were furious at my behaviour. We were a close-knit group of girls and I had been the first to have a baby. They could not under-

stand why I had not returned calls or chosen to share this time with them. I remembered the advice of my doula too late. She had told me to be clear with my friends, long before the birth, that I would not be seeing people for three weeks. "If you feel up to it sooner, then invite them around, but rather prepare them for the worst." I had not done that. Friends who had babies barely noticed my absence. When I returned they were so forgiving, just laughing it off.

Tracy had reacted the worst. It was unforgivable to her. She was going through a particularly bad patch with her relationship breaking up and felt I had cut her out of my life. After harsh words, we ended the friendship. I often think of her and miss her companionship but I also realise that, if the depth of our friendship couldn't withstand that, it would never have made it through this year.

But with her, I lost my best support system, so I have really gone through this time alone with a few new friends. It has made me stronger and more self-reliant, but I wish I had friends to share it with. It has meant I rely more and more on my husband for companionship. I feel desperate and dependent on him at times. I know I have become a needy woman, and I watch myself with loathing. Sometimes I wish I just had a life again. "Chin up," I say. "It will get better."

my story: Nomsah

In my culture, a man's place is not with his baby. This is the terrain of women and it is held by your mother. Your mother looks after both you and the baby, as if you are both newborns in need of love and nurturing.

I had my first baby at my mother's one-roomed house in a small village in Limpopo. I was eighteen at the time and two years off completing high school. We were prepared for the birth and I had my bags packed and money for the taxi on hand, when I went into labour. The clinic was a thirty-minute drive, so my mother started immediately trying to find transport. But it was nine at night and there was nothing. I knew I would have my baby at home. My mother had delivered my sister's three babies. We were both totally relaxed.

Our house has only two rooms, with an outdoor toilet, so I laboured in my mother's bedroom. The baby came fast and by midnight it was in my arms, wrapped in a blanket. My mother had lit the stove for warmth and was fuelling it with wood, as it was midwinter. She boiled up a large pot of water and I got into the zinc bath, while she tended to my baby and cleaned up. Then she bundled me into bed wrapped in warm blankets. She slept on a mattress in the room while I nursed my baby in the bed. When I finished, she would take the baby from me, feed me and lull me to sleep.

The next day, we called my boyfriend to let him know he had a daughter and he promised to come and visit her within three months. His mother came to see her granddaughter and brought her all the clothes she needed, as is the custom. Often the mother-in-law will come and stay for up to three months to ensure her grandchild is looked after and to support the mother in the early days.

My sister came to stay to help us out. I lay in bed and was cared for by my mother and sister. Their priority was to feed me up. They would take turns caring for my baby when I slept and rested.

In my culture, neither of us could leave the bedroom until the clamp on the belly-button fell. This usually takes ten to fourteen days. After that, we were allowed around the house and into the yard. But not out into the streets. That only happens after two months. After three months, I went back to school. My daughter was all of ours. She came from my body, but she was part of a larger family of women. With my second child, I was living in the city, working, and I delivered in a hospital. It was ten years later. Again we followed the same custom, but this time I brought my mother to stay with me. One day, I will do this for my daughter.

THE MIKVAH

Once a month, more and more young Jewish women are following a ritual as old as their faith. For the seven days of their periods each month they abstain from sex with their husbands. Following their periods, they count seven "white" days when there is no longer any bleeding. During this time there are no sexual relations between partners. On the seventh night, after dark, the women go to the public mikvah bath to cleanse themselves.

The build-up to the immersion is private, meticulous and ritualistic. Some women make their preparations at home where they wash their bodies and hair, remove all make up and nail varnish and trim their nails. They will enter the mikvah clean for the law of Family Purity states that nothing should come between the waters and your body. Others will make their preparations in a special area.

A woman's monthly period (niddah, a state of bloodletting) is a meeting point between life and death. It is the death of an egg, which means a potential child will not be born. The waters of the mikvah are a sign of life. The immersion signifies that the possibility of life will begin again with her next cycle. Often mikvah attendants will say to a woman as she leaves: "See you in nine months."

A woman is in a state of niddah during her postpartum bleeding. It is then, also that the faith dictates the physical boundaries between husband and wife. After seven white days, she will participate in the mikvah ritual and return home. This tradition is often misinterpreted as a confinement period, but that is not the case.

More than just symbolic, the ritual is one women adore and rising numbers of modern women are coming back to it, to sanctify marriage in a fast-paced world that holds little sacred. It is a ritual that acknowledges the different physical states a woman is in and allows her to create her own time and space within a marriage.

RESOURCES

ONLINE 'ZINES FOR HIP MOMS

Salon.com, Mothers Who Think, www.salon.com
Women24, www.women24.com
The Guardian, www.guardian.co.uk
Baby Centre, a good resource for parents www.babycentre.co.uk
iVillage, lots of resources and information www.ivillage.co.uk
Parent Centre, tips, advice and stories www.parentcentre.com
Blue Suit, for working moms www.bluesuit.com

MEDICAL HELP

Emergency Numbers
Netcare Emergency Services 082 911
MRI Criticare 0800 111 990
Medical Rescue International 011 242 0242
Emergency Medical Training 082 782 2001
St John Ambulance 011 403 4227 or 021 461 8420
SA Red Cross Society 021 797 5360
Child Accident Prevention Foundation of SA 021 685 5208
Red Cross Children's Hospital Poison Information Service
    021 685 5308
Western Province Lifesaving Association, water safety,
    resuscitation 082 826 2198
UCT Medicine Information Centre 021 448 3202
SA Medic Alert Foundation 021 461 7328
Child Accident Prevention Foundation 011 792 4332
    or 021 685 5208
Poison Information Centre 021 931 6129

ONLINE MEDICAL SITES

www.medicinenet.com
www.ecureme.com
www.explainplease.com

Homeopathy help

www.homeopathysa.co.za
www.homeopathyhome.com
www.healthy.net
www.e-homeopathy.com

Alternative health

For a full listing of alternative health practitioners and workshops pick up a Link-Up, available free at health shops nationwide.

Body and mind

The Alternative Natural Health Directory
www.bodyandmind.co.za

SAVE TIME

SHOP ONLINE
Pick 'n Pay www.picknpay.co.za
Woolworths www.woolworths.co.za

DOG WALKING
Visit your nearest vet for a dog walker or pick up a pooch magazine

NAPPY DELIVERY
Happy Nappy 011 789 8086
Wishee Washee 011 795 3831

CHILD 'TAXI' SERVICE
Serviceable Sisters 011 788 9302

NANNIES AND AU PAIRS

CAPE TOWN
Au Pair At Home 021 461 0452
Mary Poppins Child Care Training College and Placement
Service 021 674 6689
Somerset Kidz full day, half day and aftercare 021 852 1756
Super Sitters 021 439 4985
Child Minders 021 788 6788

GAUTENG

Au-Pairs-R-Us 011 464 2975

Benoni Childminders Association   011 973 2752

Choice Child Care 011 646 2718   www.choicechildcare.co.za

JCR Au Pairs and Nannies 011 464 2975   aupair@jcr.co.za

Pretoria Daymothers' Association 012 543 1862

The Governess Connection 011 883 9704

The Pink Foot Babysitting Agency 083 692 8475

The Professional Childcare College 011 482 3378

www.childcarecollege.co.za

SEX IT UP

Expanded Orgasm Workshops with Jonti Searll 083 743 5129

jontisearll@mweb.co.za

Sexologist Marlene Wasserman (aka Dr Eve)

dreve@worldonline.co.za

Visit www.amazon.com and search under erotica.

Sex shops stock a large collection of second-hand erotica and

porn novellas.

Romance Writing Workshops, The Write Co. 011 666 4766

or 083 273 2580

DANCE OR MOVE

For a list of dance schools near you, consult your Yellow Pages.

For body and spirit moves:
Nia www.niasouthafrica.co.za 021 674 3747
www.lovingtouch.co.za/nia/nia_classes.htm
Biodanza www.biodanza.co.za 011 884 6403
Capoiera http://www.capoeira.co.za/

PLAY

CAPE TOWN
Moms and Babes Workshops 021 975 6279
Mother and Child Association Workshops 021 712 3186

GAUTENG
Clamber Club 011 325 2031
Mothers and Miracles 011 395 4760 or 011 792 5760
Parent and Child Association Workshops 011 578 6864
Moms and Babes 082 898 7790 or 072 484 8208
Mummy and Me 011 455 5578
Top Tots 011 868 2489
Planning for Play 011 768 2394

CHILL

MEDITATE

National Office for Transcendental Meditation

Information Centre 011 728 0959

www.tm-online.org.za

The Triba Centre is a luxury holistic centre for mother and child opening soon in Rosebank, Johannesburg. Equipped with libraries, wireless, gyms and all pampering treatments under the sun. Check out www.tri-ba.com or call 011 788 2503.

Retreat for your soul

Buddhist Retreat Centre, Ixopo, KwaZulu Natal

039 834 1863 www.brcixopo.co.za

The Dharma Centre (Poep Kwang Sa), Head Temple, Africa, Robertson 023 626 3515

Emoyeni Retreat Centre, Rustenburg/Brits 014 574 3662

emoyeni@xsinet.co.za or www.emoyeni-retreat.com

Kagyu Samye Dzong International website: www.samyeling.org

Mahasiddha Kadampa Buddhist Centre, 60 Buckingham Road, Durban, Kloof 3610

082 443 1547 or 031 464 0983

Nan Hua Buddhist Temple,18 Fo Guang Road, Bronkhorstspruit, Gauteng

013 931 0009 or fax 013 931 0013

Rondebosch Dharma Centre (Poep Soeng Soen Won), Rondebosch, Cape Town 021 686 3698 or 021 790 5546

The Tibet Society of South Africa, Pinetown,
KZN 031 7014307 tidbnsa@iafrica.com
website: www.tibet.org.za

COUNSELLING SERVICES OR SUPPORT

Post-Natal Depression Support Association (PNDSA),
083 309 3960 or 082 882 0072 liz@pnda.co.za,
www.pndsa.co.za
Anxiety and Depression Support Group 011 783 1474
0800 567 567
Lifeline www.lifeline.org.za 0861 322 322
Life Link Pregnancy Crisis Centre, Sharon (from 9am to 1pm)
011 394 8560
SA Society of Psychiatry, 021 557 9373 www.sasop.co.za
Psychological Society of SA 011 486 3322 www.psyssa.com
Family and Marriage Association of South Africa (FAMSA)
www.famsa.org.za
National Office: 011 975 7106, 082 231 0380,
011 975 7107 or 082 231 0381

GAUTENG
SA Sexual Health Association 0860 100 262
Child and Family Centre 011 486 2890
Johannesburg Parent and Child Counselling Centre
011 484 1734

CAPE TOWN

The Parent Centre 021 762 0116

Lifeline 021 461 1111

Post-Natal Depression Support Association 021 797 4498 or

Liz Boons 082 882 0072

KWAZULU-NATAL

Child Assessment and Therapy Centre 031 208 5117

Lifeline for antenatal depression 031 303 2222

Father Massima 031 201 1288

PARENTING COURSES

GAUTENG

EduBabe: Domestic, Parenting and Nanny Training

011 768 0359

Effective Parenting, A CD-based course

www.effectiveparenting.co.za or 011 786 5516

Soul Parenting Course, The Academy of Metaphysics

011 708 0000 www.metaphysics.co.za

Family Dynamics Course, The Academy of Metaphysics

011 708 0000

www.metaphysics.co.za

CAPE TOWN

The Parent Centre, 021 762 0116

Joyful Child Workshops, Cape Town, 021 557 3878 or

082 927 5714 or www.joyology.co.za

DURBAN

Joyful Child Workshops 031 765 6159 or 083 566 5051 or
www.joyology.co.za

WEBSITES

Baby Assist www.babyassist.co.za for advice on pregnancy,
childbirth and childcare

Babynet www.babynet.co.za plenty here to guide you through
pregnancy, birth and early childcare

BREASTFEEDING HELP

Many large pharmacies have a nursing sister who holds a clinic
once a week and will give breastfeeding advice as well as dispensing inoculations and general advice.

All clinics run a similar programme, so call one nearest to you.

The clinic where you gave birth can refer you to a breastfeeding consultant who will come to your home and support you with
latching and problems.

La Leche League, South Africa is part of the International
Division of La Leche League International. It is a nonprofit, non-
sectarian volunteer organisation dedicated to providing information, encouragement and support to breastfeeding mothers
through its unique mother-to-mother support network. The website has listings to all national support offices.

www.lalecheleague.org/SouthAfrica.html

GAUTENG

La Leche League SA 011 475 5837

East Rand 011 795 4204

The Baby Business 011 783 0411 Anne Richardson – breast-feeding consultant

Brenda's Lactation Education Support Services 011 480 4000

CAPE TOWN

Breastfeeding Association 021 686 8363

Cape Town Breastfeeding Liason Group 021 460 9264

La Leche League 021 910 0606

Sister Sue's Mother and Child Clinic Table View 021 556 2024

The Lactation Consultancy 021 557 2032

SUPPORT GROUPS

Single Moms Support Group, Monica Spiro 021 794 1577

Teenage Pregnancy Support Group 012 343 6401

Hyperactive Support Group, national office 011 887 655

SA Multiple Births Association, contact info on 10118 for a number in your area

WELL BABY CLINICS

There are thousands of these clinics nationwide with nursing sisters who will advise you on vaccinations, baby health and your health as well as support you with breastfeeding. Some are located in large pharmacies while others are home-based practices that offer both antenatal and post-natal support. Many of them offer exercise classes, massage lessons and a "moms and babes" weekly tea group and are invaluable for advice, support and social contact. As a first base, buy a recent pregnancy or baby magazine and check out their listings for a sister near you.

Otherwise, contact the nearest clinic with a maternity ward and ask for the nearest well baby clinic.

All contact details were correct at the time of going to print.

ABOUT THE AUTHOR

Sarah Bullen is a journalist, editor and documentary maker. She gained 20kgs in her first pregnancy, popped her baby – daughter Ruby – out in three hours and spent the next 12 months doggedly working her way through every tip in a bid to return to her former glory. She has just given birth to her second baby, and this time around she is armed (and, hopefully, less dangerous).

NOTES

Oshun

Published by Oshun Books
an imprint of Struik Publishers
(a division of New Holland Publishing (South Africa) (Pty) Ltd)
PO Box 1144, Cape Town, 8000
New Holland Publishing is a member of Johnnic Communications Ltd

First published 2005
1 3 5 7 9 10 8 6 4 2
Publication © Oshun Books 2005
Text © Sarah Bullen
Cover image © Gallo Images/gettyimages.com

PUBLISHING MANAGER: Michelle Matthews
EDITOR: Anne Taylor
PROOFREADER: Vanessa Weyer
TEXT DESIGN AND TYPESETTING: Beverley Dodd
PRODUCTION CONTROLLER: Valerie Kommer

Set in 8.5 pt on 15 pt TradeGothic
Reproduction by Hirt & Carter (Cape) (Pty) Ltd
Printed and bound by Paarl Print, Oosterland Street, Paarl, South Africa

ISBN 1 77007 035 4
www.oshunbooks.co.za

IMAGES OF AFRICA
PHOTO LIBRARY

Log on to our photographic website www.imagesofafrica.co.za for an African experience